T0290201

MG MAGNETTE

PAUL BATHO

AMBERLEY

First published 2019

Amberley Publishing
The Hill, Stroud,
Gloucestershire, GL5 4EP

www.amberley-books.com

ISBN: 978 1 4456 8603 5 (print)
ISBN: 978 1 4456 8604 2 (ebook)

British Library Cataloguing in Publication Data.
A catalogue record for this book is available from the British Library.

Typeset in 10pt on 13pt Celeste.
Origination by Amberley Publishing.
Printed in the UK.

Contents

1 The MG Story – Performance with Style for the Common Man   4

2 MGs with a Roof – The Magnette Heritage   12

3 Gerald Palmer   18

4 Magnette Gestation and Birth   25

5 The Magnette Meets the Market   36

6 Growing Up and Growing Old – Production Changes 1954–58   40

7 Improving the Breed   53

8 Racing and Rallying   62

9 Renaissance   69

10 Magnettes in the Twenty-first Century   75

Appendix 1   86

Appendix 2   88

Appendix 3   89

Appendix 4   91

Bibliography   94

Acknowledgements   95

1

The MG Story – Performance with Style for the Common Man

Motoring for the Masses

The early 1920s was a pivotal period in the history of the motor industry. The world was recovering from the trauma of the First World War and a new, post-war generation had very different hopes and aspirations from those that existed in 1914. Car manufacturers had to adapt to the demands of a new world.

The seeds of change had been planted before the war in Detroit, Michigan, when Henry Ford began to produce his Model T in 1908. Early motoring was strictly for the wealthy enthusiast but Ford's genius was to recognise that there was a huge market among the less well-heeled, if only cars could be produced more cheaply. By introducing production line techniques and rigorously rationalising components, Ford drove the price of his Model T down from $825 in 1908 to $440 in 1914, while annual production increased from 10,700 to 203,000. By 1914, Ford had captured nearly 50 per cent of the entire US market.

Ford's success did not go unnoticed in the UK. In 1912 William Morris, who had begun his career repairing bicycles in Oxford and progressed to motorcycle and car manufacture, built a new factory in Cowley, on the outskirts of Oxford, to produce his new Morris Oxford. With its famous 'bull-nose' radiator to the fore, and an attractive price of £165, the Oxford (and its cheaper stablemate the Cowley) rapidly established itself as the transport of choice for the aspiring middle classes. Annual sales figures rocketed from 393 in 1913 to 54,000 in 1925. Morris's main UK rival, Herbert Austin, was not far behind. His Austin 7 was introduced in 1922 and went on to sell 290,000 by 1939.

At the other end of the scale, wealthier motorists were still well catered for. Many manufacturers would sell a 'chassis' (basically the entire car minus bodywork), leaving the purchaser to engage one of the many traditional coachbuilders to clothe it in whatever bodywork he or she desired. The millionaire Howard Hughes, for example, spent $13,450 on a Rolls-Royce Silver Ghost with US Springfield bodywork in 1925 – the cost of fifty

The original Morris Cowley of 1913. (Photo courtesy of the Mike Allison Collection)

Model Ts! Many other upmarket manufacturers adopted the same approach: Bentley, Hispano-Suiza, Napier, Sunbeam, Daimler and others competed to provide the wealthy with stylish transport.

Some motorists, though, could only dream of a Rolls or Bentley, but aspired to driving something a little more glamorous than the run-of-the-mill Morris or Austin. In the frenzy of the post-war manufacturing boom, this important middle-ground market had been largely overlooked.

MG – The Early Days

Enter Cecil Kimber. Born in Dulwich, London, in 1888, the family moved to Lancashire in around 1896 when his father opened a printing ink business there. Kimber was an enthusiastic motorcycle pioneer but an accident left him with a badly broken leg and a permanent limp, so he turned to four wheels, starting with a 1912 Singer 10. His leg injury meant that he was unfit to serve in the First World War and he worked for his father's firm until a disagreement caused him to leave and find his true calling in the motor industry. Starting with the Yorkshire car manufacturer Sheffield-Simplex, he moved on to A. C. Cars in Thames Ditton, Surrey, and then to E. G. Wrigley Ltd of Birmingham, who supplied components to many of the UK motor manufacturers. But with Wrigley heading towards bankruptcy another move was needed, and in 1921 Kimber was appointed sales manager of Morris Garages in Oxford.

Morris Garages had been set up in 1911 by William Morris as a dealership for his own and other manufacturers' cars. With the rapid growth in production, Morris handed the running of Morris Garages to Edward Armstead in 1919. Armstead appointed Kimber as sales manager but abruptly resigned in March 1922 before taking his own life. Aged thirty-four, Kimber found himself promoted to general manager.

By then, Kimber had some eight years' experience in the motor industry in a variety of roles but he lacked any formal qualifications. Nevertheless, by all accounts he was

5

Cecil Kimber at his desk in Abingdon. (Photo courtesy of MGCC)

an effective – some suggest ruthless – businessman with a strong innovative streak, characteristics which had doubtless impressed William Morris.

In his new position, it seems Kimber had a fair degree of autonomy. Recognising the potential demand for something with a bit more pizzazz than the standard Morris products, and probably inspired by the short-lived Cowley Super Sports of 1921, he began to design special bodywork which could be fitted to the standard Morris chassis.

By early 1923, small-scale production of a version of the 'Morris Garages Chummy' began, based on the Morris Cowley but with much more attractive bodywork by Carbodies of Coventry. Production reached twenty cars a month, assembled by around half a dozen men in a small works in Alfred Lane, Oxford. Later that year an alternative and rather stylish open two-seater body by a local coachbuilder, Raworth of Oxford, was offered. This sold at £350, more than twice the price a standard Cowley.

Kimber's Morris Garages seem to have experimented with a variety of body styles during 1924. Advertisements refer to open two- and four-seaters, a 'vee-front' saloon and a landaulette. The numbers sold seem to have been relatively small but in May an advertisement for the 'MG Super Sports Morris' in the *Morris Owner* magazine was the first to feature the famous MG octagonal badge.

The launch of the 1925 MG 14/28, based on the new Oxford chassis, marked a big step forward. Available as an open two- or four-seater or with a variety of saloon bodies, it featured a longer bonnet topped with jaunty nautical air scoops, the wings had a graceful line and it could be ordered in a range of fashionable colours. The new car also began to distance itself from its prosaic cousin mechanically. Flattened springs reduced the ride height, modifications to the steering sharpened the handling and engines were mildly tuned. The motoring press praised the new model and sales took off.

In 1926, after 400 14/28s had been produced, Morris introduced a new Oxford which featured a flat, angular radiator in place of the distinctive bull-nose of earlier models, so the MG version, known as the 14/40, had to follow suit. Kimber's MGs were becoming recognised as something slightly different, and more stylish, than the bread-and-butter cars of the day, while remaining much cheaper than the luxury brands to which MG owners probably aspired. As a result, some 900 14/40s were sold over the next three years.

The Morris Sports Cowley of 1921 lasted only one season but was an inspiration for the MG range from 1924. (Photo courtesy of the Mike Allison Collection)

The MG 14/40, introduced in 1926, sold in significant numbers and helped to create MG's distinct market niche. (Photo courtesy of MGCC)

MG Grows Up

The MG Car Company was established in the spring of 1928 as a wholly owned subsidiary of Morris Garages Ltd. As a sign of its growing independence, the company unveiled two completely new models at the 1928 London Motor Show in October – the MG 18/80 Six, a substantial and well appointed sports tourer, and its baby sister, the M-type Midget Sports.

Both models sported a new and distinctive style of radiator which, with its centrally mounted octagonal badge and prominent central bar, would distinguish nearly all MG models for the next three-quarters of a century.

Unlike previous models, the 18/80 was built on MG's own chassis and its six-cylinder, 2,468cc engine, though based on a Morris design, was substantially modified. It was a powerful car by the standards of the day, and with a top speed of 80 mph it out-performed equivalent models from distinguished marques such as Alvis and Lagonda. Customers could buy the chassis for £420, which compared favourably with Alvis's offering at £500 and was less than half the price of the 3-litre Bentley chassis which cost an imposing £925. MG was moving into a rather more exclusive market segment but the principle of providing value for money remained.

The 18/80 provided the glamour but in the longer term the Midget, a tiny two-seater sports car with a clever 847cc overhead camshaft engine, would turn out to be the more significant. *The Autocar* magazine commented that 'The MG Midget will make sports car history', and it was right – Midgets were produced by MG for most of the next fifty-two years.

Without the Midget, MG would have almost certainly gone the way of so many small manufacturers producing specialist cars following the Wall Street Crash in

The MG 18/80 of 1928 was the first model to be built on MG's own chassis and was a worthy rival for some of the longer-established manufacturers of high-performance cars. (Photo courtesy of MGCC)

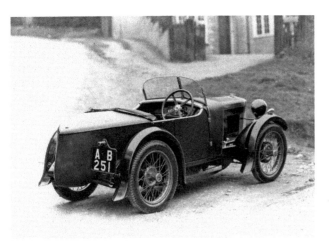

The MG M-type Midget – the first of a long line of Midgets. (Photo courtesy of MGCC)

October 1929. The market for large, powerful and expensive cars evaporated; even the once mighty Bentley succumbed to the receivers in July 1931. Sales figures emphasise the point: MG only ever produced 736 18/80s, while 3,235 M-type Midgets were sold between 1928 and 1932.

The Triple-M Years and the First Magnettes

From 1929 to 1935 MG developed an enormous range of small sports cars. The original M-type spawned the C, D, J, P, Q and R-type Midgets, all four-cylinder cars with small but technically advanced overhead camshaft engines. The first six-cylinder car of the line was the 1931 F-type with a capacity of 1,271cc and, as a larger car, it is not surprising that Kimber chose to call it the Magna. The following year, a smaller-engined (1,087cc), six-cylinder model, the K-type, was introduced, so the name Magnette probably seemed the logical choice, pitched as it was between the Midget and the Magna. It was certainly not the last time a manufacturer looked beyond the confines of a dictionary to name a product! Midget, Magnette and Magna – no surprise, then, that the iconic cars of this era became collectively known as the Triple-M MGs.

K3 Magnettes during the Italian Mille Miglia race in 1933 when the team won the 1100 class and the Team Award against strong opposition. (Photo courtesy of the Mike Allison Collection)

Driving K3 Magnettes, the MG team won the 1933 Ards TT. Tazio Nuvolari and Alec Hounslow look pleased with their success while Chief Mechanic Reg Jackson realizes his boots need re-shining! (Photo courtesy of the Mike Allison Collection)

The frenetic course of development was spurred on by fierce competition on racetracks, in rallies and in trials in the UK and abroad. MGs soon became the cars to beat in their class. Leading the pack was the K3 Magnette, probably the most famous racing MG of all. A 1st and 2nd in class in its first major event, the 1933 Mille Miglia, set the scene for an impressive haul of trophies over the next two years.

Spurred on by MG's competition successes, the J- and P-type Midgets came to epitomise the transport of the dashing young chaps of the period. Around 2,500 of each were sold – good numbers for the time – but sales of almost all the other models were in the hundreds or fewer. It was a complex business model which could not last.

Corporatism

In 1935 William Morris, by then Lord Nuffield, called time on MG's semi-independent status. The MG Car Company Ltd was sold to Morris Motors Ltd and Cecil Kimber's authority was curtailed under a new management regime, initially headed by Leonard Lord. The works competition department was, despite its extraordinary successes, disbanded and a new range of cars was introduced comprising just one sports car, the TA Midget, and two larger cars, the 1.5-litre VA and the 2.3-litre SA, which were available in a range of saloon and open body styles. The even bigger 2.6-litre WA followed in 1938.

Under Leonard Lord, the balance sheet took priority over engineering innovation and the new cars reflected this. The engines, drive train and other key components originated from the parent group and were employed in MG products with only limited modifications. The new range included some excellent motorcars but some of the romance had been sacrificed to the corporate god of profit.

Thus began a new business model for MG which, in essence, was to remain unchanged right through to the early twenty-first century. Immediately post-war, the T-type Midget line continued until 1955 and was supplemented by the new Y-type saloon, both cars

The handsome 1938 MG WA saloon – a big, stylish but stately saloon – was one of the models representing an abrupt change of direction for MG from 1935. (Photo courtesy of MGCC)

using many components from the Nuffield Group, as Morris Motors Ltd had become after its merger with Riley in 1938. The MGA sports car and Z-type Magnette saloon which succeeded them both had, as is described later, mildly modified engines from the British Motor Corporation (BMC), Nuffield's successor. In the early 1960s the trend was continued with the new Midgets and MGBs, which were produced right through to 1980 when the MG factory in Abingdon finally closed its doors.

MG after Abingdon

Even though its famous factory was no more, the MG brand was too valuable to be allowed to disappear altogether. British Leyland, the conglomerate organisation formed following the merger of BMC and Leyland Motors in 1968, revived the MG badge on hotted-up versions of the Austin Metro, Maestro and Montego models from 1982. Despite harrumphing from dyed-in-the-wool enthusiasts, these were well-received cars and in many ways their concept harked back to the very first MG – they were mildly modified versions of a large corporation's product, designed to appeal to the buyer looking for something just that little bit different.

To true MG fans, a more exciting development came in the form of the 1995 MGF, produced by yet another incarnation of the old Nuffield Corporation, the Rover Group. This was a brand-new, contemporary mid-engined sports two-seater whose design appeared at first glance to borrow nothing from mainstream models – until one looked a little closer and noticed the corporate K-series engine and the Austin Metro sub-frames.

In the spring of 2001 a new range of MG sporting saloons, the ZR, ZS and ZT, was launched, closely based on the contemporary Rover 25, 45 and 75 models but with enhanced performance, revised suspension settings and mildly modified bodywork bedecked with MG badges. This turned out to be the final throw of the dice for MG's seventy-seven-year-old mission to create a swifter, sexier version of a humdrum product. They were good cars but it was not to last; in 2005 MG Rover became insolvent. Administrators were appointed and the remaining assets were sold to the Nanjing Automobile Group of China. But for eight decades, Kimber's formula had stood the test of time and made the initials MG famous throughout the world.

Rebirth. The 1995 MGF was a continuation of a long tradition of MGs – something a bit special, but still ingeniously crafted from corporate components. (Photo courtesy of MGCC)

2

MGs with a Roof –
The Magnette Heritage

In terms of brand recognition, MG is right up there with the likes of BMW, Mercedes-Benz, Hoover and Coca-Cola – an astonishing achievement for a small manufacturer based in an obscure corner of England. Ask just about anyone with the slightest smidgen of knowledge about motorcars to describe an MG and they will picture a small, open two-seater piloted at speed by a debonair young fellow, his passenger's blonde mane flowing in the slipstream – maybe not a vision meeting universal approval in an age of gender equality, but then MGs are often the subject of sepia-tinted nostalgia.

But perception and reality differ. Right at the start, in 1924 a publicity shot showed Rene Kimber stepping gracefully from the cosy interior of a Morris Garages saloon car and production records show that, over the entire production run of UK-produced MGs from Oxford and Abingdon, totalling around 1.1 million cars, around one-third had a fixed roof. Sometimes (between 1936 and 1939, in 1954/5 and for most of the post-Abingdon period from 1980) saloon production substantially eclipsed that of two-seater sports cars.

The Birth of the Sports Saloon

Though Cecil Kimber had no formal training, he did know a thing or two about marketing. His business plan from the start was to make a car that was 10 per cent better than the model on which it was based but which sold at a 50 per cent price premium. Kimber's engineering modifications to Cowleys and Oxfords could fairly be described as modest but by including the word 'Sports' in the model's name – or better still, 'Super Sports' – his cars acquired a magical aura which persuaded buyers to dig deeper into their pockets.

And if the magic worked, why limit it to open two-seaters? MG saloons were produced from the company's beginnings and most featured exceptionally comfortable interiors with sumptuous leather upholstery, carpeting and nicely finished wood veneers. However, very few have survived – saloon bodywork of the time was notoriously prone to cracking, leaks and rot in the timber frame, leading to its rapid disintegration.

These early MG saloons were among the very first examples of a new genre of motorcar, the 'sports saloon'. The term defies a neat classification, which has meant it has been misapplied to some very undeserving products over the years, but ever since the mid-1920s there has been a clear demand for cars that combine above-average performance and handling with the extra comfort offered by a snug, enclosed cabin.

The first MG sports saloon: this 1925 MG 14/28 Super Sports Salonette demonstrates what a little Kimber magic could do to the humble Morris Oxford. This car is the sole survivor of six fitted with the unusual 'duck-tailed' salonette body by Carbodies of Coventry. (Photo courtesy of Vintage & Prestige Classic Cars Ltd)

The sumptuously trimmed interior of the Super Sports Salonette. (Photo courtesy of Vintage & Prestige Classic Cars Ltd)

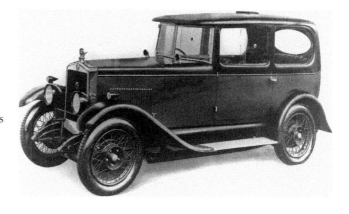

A 1927 MG 14/40 Super Sports Morris Oxford Salonette demonstrates the new 'flat nose' Morris radiator. (Photo courtesy of the Mike Allison Collection)

The MG 'Six' four-door saloon prototype of 1928/9. The car was launched as the '18/80' at the London Motor Show. Note the painted-on spinners in anticipation of the Rudge-Whitworth wheels which had yet to be supplied! (Photo courtesy of the Mike Allison Collection)

The beautifully fitted interior of the MG 18/80 Six, with ample space for four adults and their luggage. (Photo courtesy of the Mike Allison Collection)

The first Magnette model, the K1, powered by a 1,087cc OHC six-cylinder engine and introduced at the 1932 London Motor Show. This example is the 'pillarless saloon'. It won few friends, as it needed hard driving to obtain the performance available, and suffered, like most early saloon cars, from water leakage in wet weather. (Photo courtesy of the Mike Allison Collection)

The prototype K1 Magnette at the top of Beggars Roost hill, in Devon, with H. S. Linfield of *The Light Car* magazine, who tested the car. Though many criticised its performance, Linfield gave it a good write-up. (Photo courtesy of the Mike Allison Collection)

The first MG designed 'in-house' – the 18/80 Six of 1928 – was offered from the start with open tourer bodywork or as a two- or four-door saloon, and two-thirds of the 258 customers in the first year of production chose a fixed roof. These were fast but luxurious vehicles – no wind in the hair and flies in the teeth for the owners of MG 18/80 saloons and yet their 'sports' pedigree is undeniable.

During the Triple-M years, however, MG largely turned away from saloon production. Although closed versions of the F- and L-type Magnas and the K-type Magnette were offered by the factory, these cars were really coupés providing rear seats for occasional use rather than full-sized saloons; the vast majority of Triple-M cars were open two- and four-seater sports models.

MG Sports Saloons – Establishing a Tradition

The rigours of corporate discipline imposed on MG when the MG Car Company Ltd was sold to Morris Motors Ltd in 1935 enforced product rationalisation and brought about the re-emergence of genuine saloon cars from the Abingdon factory. Such a move was supported by market trends. The sports saloon concept had matured during the early 1930s while MG were concentrating almost exclusively on open sports cars, so by 1935 the company had some catching up to do.

MG's rival, Riley, had spotted the potential for a saloon with just a tad more glamour with its 9 hp model of 1928 – a car which spawned a series of derivatives over the following decade. The Riley 9 Kestrel and Falcon models suggested speed and agility while the Adelphi, Biarritz and Monaco gave more than a hint of style and glamour to a relatively inexpensive car. Rover joined in after a 1930 Rover Light Six saloon raced and beat the exotic 'Blue Train' from the Riviera to Paris, a stunt which gave a fillip to a manufacturer with a reputation for producing sturdy but unexciting cars.

MG was therefore a bit late to the party with its new range of saloons, which began with the launch of the 2.3-litre SA for the 1936 model year, and continued with the smaller 1½-litre VA in 1937. However, their introduction, and that of the 1938 2.6-litre WA, represented a sharp about-turn for the company's products. Sports cars they were not, but by a combination of performance, style and MG heritage they thoroughly deserved the elusive 'sports saloon' moniker.

MG was no longer a pioneer of sports car design but the company's foray into the world of luxuriously appointed sporting saloons and tourers was a commercial success – VA, SA and WA sales totalled more than 5,500 between 1936 and 1939 compared with 3,382 of the contemporary TA and TB Midget sports cars. But the events of September 1939 put paid to car manufacture as the Abingdon factory was turned over to the production of aircraft components and tanks for the duration of the war.

Before the war started, work was already well underway for a new MG saloon car. It was relatively small by comparison with its predecessors, and utilised a bodyshell derived from the 1938 Morris 8 Series E and a four-cylinder 1250cc engine developed from the Morris 10. The new model was designed to compete with the smaller sports saloons from Triumph, Singer, Riley and Talbot. In a further break from tradition, it was the first MG to be designed without input from Cecil Kimber.

The new saloon nevertheless retained enough unique features to qualify as a genuine MG. It was one of the first British production cars to be fitted with independent front suspension and rack and pinion steering, thus offering much tauter handling than the majority of contemporary saloon cars, while the bodywork featured the distinctive MG radiator grille to the fore, flowing wing lines and an elegant swept tail which skilfully disguised its humble Morris origins.

The MG 1¼-litre Y-type (as it became officially known) finally entered production in early 1947. With petrol on ration until 1950 and in a period of post-war austerity, small economical cars were in demand, so MG's more modest new offering fitted the bill. At the same time, with its distinctive lines and an interior rich in leather and walnut veneer, the car harked back to more affluent times and appealed to the slightly better-heeled customer. A total of 6,158 saloons were produced from 1947 to 1951, when the original YA was superseded by the lightly modified YB. By the time production ceased in August 1953, close to 7,500 Y-type saloons had been built – nearly three times more than any previous MG saloon car.

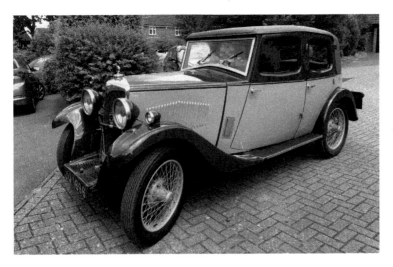

The many variants of the Riley 9 represented some of the very best mid-1930s sports saloons. This is a 1933 Monaco. (Photo courtesy of Robin Lawton)

By the early 1950s, however, the pre-war charms of the Y-type were fading as rival manufacturers introduced new models incorporating post-war technological advances and the latest, streamlined, full-width bodywork. It was time for MG to put aside its traditions and enter the modern era.

The 'corporate' face of MG (left to right): a 2.6-litre WA saloon, a 1.5-litre VA tourer, and a 2-litre SA saloon. Stately and elegant cars, the SVW range was a big contrast to previous models. (Photo courtesy of MGCC SVW Register)

Y-type bodies being trimmed on the line in Abingdon – apparently not a job for the men! (Photo courtesy of the MGCC Y Register)

The last of MG's pre-war designs and a study in classical elegance – a 1952 YB saloon. (Photo courtesy of Neil Cairns)

3

Gerald Palmer

A Man with a Passion

Gerald Marley Palmer was born in 1911 in England but grew up in Southern Rhodesia, now Zimbabwe, after his father, Will, was appointed district engineer for the Beira, Mashonaland & Rhodesia Railway. This was a vital supply line in the First World War to the British and South African troops in the campaign against German forces in Tanganyika, at that time a German colony. One of Palmer's earliest memories, aged six, was of the rebuilding of a steel railway bridge after it had been washed away in a storm. An exciting environment in which to be brought up and one in which engineering was very much to the fore.

Gerald Marley Palmer (1911–99) pictured in 1942. (Photo courtesy of Celia Palmer)

Gerald Palmer's first foray into car design – his rebodied Model T Ford of 1925/6. (Photo courtesy of Celia Palmer)

Palmer's passion for cars was evident from an early age. His talent for car design took flight at the age of fourteen when his parents gave him free reign to restyle their old Ford Model T after it was replaced with a new car. In his autobiography[1], he explained how he set about the job with youthful gusto:

> I seized the Model T Ford, ripped off its bodywork, and spent all my spare time in building on it a rakish, two-seater sports body, plywood panelled and inspired by an exotic Scripps-Booth with a boat-tailed body owned by a local enthusiast. This was my first essay in motor body design and construction and it was not looked on with favour by my schoolmasters, who said it distracted from my studies.

A further distraction, according to Palmer's daughter Celia[2], were the brochures from Italian car manufacturers and stylists which Palmer ordered and pored over, again at the expense of his academic studies. Teachers may have despaired, but the die was cast.

His father would have preferred Gerald to have studied architecture but his passion and talent for vehicle design could not be ignored. Palmer sailed for England in 1927 to begin a five-year apprenticeship with the specialist commercial vehicle builder Scammell Lorries Ltd.

1. Quoted in *Auto-Architect – The Autobiography of Gerald Palmer*.
2. Interview with the author, 2018.

Developing a Natural Talent

Palmer's mentor and inspiration was Scammell's Chief Engineer, O. D. North. North was a largely unsung engineering genius of his day and appears to have been particularly suited to Scammell, whose work included creating one-off solutions to unique transport problems. Articulated vehicles for the transport of liquids and heavy machinery were a speciality, as were four- and six-wheel-drive trucks for off-road work. One of North's best-known designs was the Scammell Mechanical Horse (later known as the Scarab), a three-wheel tractor unit and trailer which revolutionised the transport of goods in confined areas such as station yards and docks. Produced from 1931 to 1968, the Mechanical Horse was a familiar sight around towns in the UK for more than four decades.

His apprenticeship with Scammell provided Palmer with unparalleled training in heavy vehicle engineering but he was keen to employ his skills in the area of his true passion – car design. In the mid-1930s he was offered an intriguing opportunity by a wealthy sponsor, Anthony Fisher, to build a sports car prototype for Joan Richmond, the Australian racing and rally driver. If successful, the prototype was to form the basis for a production model. Working with Chalenor Barson, a fellow graduate of the Institute of Automobile Engineers, a prototype car was built in a rented garage in Penge, south-east London, with Palmer doing the design work in his spare time (while still working in the Scammell drawing office) and Barson working full-time building the car.

Palmer's design incorporated some radical features. At a time when most manufacturers favoured solid axles mounted on stiff leaf springs attached to a flexible chassis, Palmer set off in the opposite direction and created a car built around a stiff chassis structure and featuring four-wheel independent suspension that provided a much more compliant ride and better roadholding – exactly the route followed by post-war designers.

Palmer's Deroy sports car of 1937 featured nicely proportioned bodywork and a sophisticated chassis. (Photo courtesy of Celia Palmer)

The Deroy featured several touches demonstrating Palmer's design ingenuity – this is the combined hood support and cover. (Photo courtesy of Celia Palmer)

The Deroy's De Dion rear suspension was very advanced for its day. (Photo courtesy of Celia Palmer)

The new car was named the Deroy, which had been the name of a tin mine owned by Palmer's father in Mozambique. The advanced chassis was clothed with a stylish two-seater body of Palmer's design. A clever touch was the ingenious hood, supported on a metal panel which served as a neat cover when the hood was stowed. It seems that performance was the only area in which the car disappointed: for reasons of cost and availability the Deroy was fitted with a side valve 1.5-litre engine used in the Scammell Mechanical Horse and this proved insufficient for a car whose looks shouted speed. When talks with Aston Martin and AC to manufacture a production model came to naught, and without the prospect of finance to develop the car further, the Deroy Car Company was wound up in 1938, with Palmer taking the car for his own use in compensation.

Into the Mainstream

Though the Deroy proved to be an unsuccessful venture commercially, it was to be the key that opened the door to Palmer's future career. In 1939, seeking a way into the mainstream motor industry, he was offered an interview by Cecil Kimber at MG. Palmer drove to Abingdon in his Deroy, whose design greatly impressed Kimber. By this stage, though, MG design had been relocated to Cowley and so, unable to offer Palmer a job at Abingdon, Kimber contacted the Morris Technical Director, A. V. Oak, who promptly offered him the position as head of MG design in the Morris drawing office.

His first job was to work on the front suspension for the planned Y-type MG. Ironically, given his championing of independent suspension, Palmer was asked to amend the original plans for an independent set-up back to a cruder but cheaper beam axle design on leaf springs – a decision which was reversed again by the time the Y-type finally reached production in 1947. But with the outbreak of war in September 1939, almost all work on civilian vehicles ceased and Palmer was reassigned to work on the de Haviland Tiger Moth trainer which was to be manufactured at Cowley. This was followed by an assignment designing the Oxford Vaporiser, a portable anaesthetic apparatus for military use.

Having moved to Morris to get into the motor industry, Palmer may have found the restrictions of war work frustrating, so when an advertisement appeared in the motoring press for a chief designer for an unnamed motor manufacturer, his curiosity was aroused and he submitted an application.

The Jowett Javelin

The manufacturer turned out to be Jowett, a long-established but relatively small company based in Bradford which had been producing light cars and commercial vehicles since 1910. Like Morris, the factory's production had been turned over to support the war effort by manufacturing artillery, ammunition and generators, but the managing director, Charles Calcott Reilly, had an eye on post-war activity. He wanted Jowett to be first out of the starting blocks with a new car that was a radical change from the company's traditional offerings, which were better known for sturdy reliability than innovation and style. Enticed by the prospect of having free rein to design a new car from scratch, and by an increase in salary from £325 to £500 a year, Palmer moved to Bradford in 1942.

His ambition was to produce a car that could accommodate six passengers and their luggage within compact dimensions while providing above average performance and good fuel economy. Light weight was important and, as the car would be aimed at markets across the world, it would require good ground clearance and the strength to cope with unsurfaced roads.

After four years of hard work and intensive testing the new Jowett Javelin was launched into a car-starved world in July 1946. It was a radical new design both for Jowett and the car industry as a whole, being strongly influenced by the work in the USA of John Tjaarda, whose 'teardrop' styling concepts were taken up by Ford and developed into the 1930s Lincoln-Zephyr. The Javelin prototype was unveiled at the Society of Motor Manufacturers and Traders display and cavalcade in London on 27 July 1946. The crowds would have been astounded that such a svelte machine could have come out of Jowett's Bradford factory.

Beneath the skin, the Javelin was powered by a modified version of Jowett's flat-four engine and incorporated independent front suspension of Palmer's own design. Contemporary road tests were enthusiastic, with *The Autocar* commenting, 'The suspension is of exceptional merit, giving a smooth ride without any tendency to pitching. The Javelin can be summed up as possessing an extremely lively performance for a car of 1.5 litres.' *The Motor*'s test came to the conclusion that the Javelin was 'unrivalled in its own field'.

The car's performance, coupled with its roadholding and handling prowess, resulted in some unexpected sporting successes, given that it had not been designed with competition in mind. With Palmer as one of two co-drivers, a Javelin won its class and the Riviera Cup in the 1949 Monte Carlo Rally. This was followed by victory in the touring car class at the 1949 Spa-Francorchamps 24-hour race and further rallying successes, notably a class win in the 1952 RAC Rally and overall victory in the 1953 Tulip Rally.

The American Lincoln-Zephyr set a new and much-copied standard for US car styling in the late 1930s. This is a 1939 model – the influences on Palmer's Javelin are clear. (Photo courtesy of Kelly McClain)

Return to Cowley

Despite the Javelin's success, Jowett remained a small operation and lacked the resources to grow. Palmer's work with the firm was done, and in July 1949 he returned to Cowley as a director with a senior design role in the Nuffield organisation.

Though his new role was important, his resources were, by modern standards, modest. In the twenty-first century, the chief designer of a new model will lead a team of perhaps twenty-five to forty skilled specialists, all using the latest design software. Marketing experts and customer liaison groups will keep the team focussed on exactly what the buying public is demanding.

Back in 1942 in Bradford, Palmer had been provided with a small office, a drawing board and a layout table, from which he, later helped by three staff, designed the entire Jowett Javelin – exterior, interior, mechanical components and all. In his new role at Nuffield, Palmer was given a desk in a shared office (next door to Alex Issigonis, designer of the Morris Minor and Mini) and a small team of ten. He was to be responsible for the design of Nuffield's future MG, Riley and Wolseley saloons but only given the vaguest hints as to what Nuffield was really looking for. As he said in an interview with Graham Robson in 1977[3]: 'Looking back, it's extraordinary to me that I was given so little briefing. Nuffield just wanted a new MG saloon and a Riley saloon to replace the RM, with no time targets and no size targets. No designer could have asked for more!'

He may have had only limited resources and the vaguest instructions from his bosses but he had one great strength, demonstrated in everything he did. This was what he modestly described (when talking about the Javelin) as 'a quite good feel for "eye-able" shapes',[4] something that was to stand him in very good stead over the next six years.

A contemporary shot of a 1952 Javelin in an evocative location in Sleights, North Yorkshire. (Photo courtesy of Noel Stokoe)

3. Interview with Graham Robson published in *Thoroughbred & Classic Cars* magazine, September 1977.
4. From Gerald Palmer's obituary in *The Independent,* 16 July 1999.

4

Magnette Gestation and Birth

Palmer's Brief

By 1949, much of Nuffield's product range was in urgent need of modernisation. The car-buying public, both in the UK and in the major export markets, was no longer prepared to accept the pre-war models which had re-emerged in 1945 from factories that had spent six years developing military hardware. People wanted something new. On top of this, the Nuffield Group had its own particular problems arising from its origins as an amalgam of several previously competing manufacturers, each with its own model range and band of loyal customers. Some serious rationalisation was needed.

Nuffield's resources had initially been concentrated on modernising the bread-and-butter products, with some success: Issigonis's radical Morris Minor had been launched to considerable acclaim in 1948 and was selling very well. Its big brothers, the four-cylinder Oxford MO-series and the Morris Six, were larger cars in the same style. Next, the more upmarket range of cars required attention.

The Wolseley range was renowned for being the favoured transport of the respectable middle classes – bank managers, senior civil servants and bishops – and was much used by the police. The new large Morrises, the Oxford and Six, had spawned Wolseley derivatives, the 4/50 and 6/80, which boasted traditional wood-and-leather interior finishes in the style expected by the more affluent buyers to whom they were targeted but, aft of the traditional upright Wolseley radiator grille, their appearance was all too similar to that of their lesser Morris siblings. Loyal customers expected their Wolseley to be a little more distinctive.

Meanwhile Riley's RM-series 1½- and 2½-litre saloons were elegant and luxurious cars that had been launched in 1945. The RM was the final design of the old independent Riley company prior to its takeover by Morris in 1938 and thus not only had pre-war origins, but also had little in common with the products of the new parent company. With the MG Y-type saloon also being a pre-war design, Palmer's brief, though vague, was key to the future of an important part of the Nuffield empire.

Nuffield's directors had identified a need for two Wolseley saloons, a four- and a six-seater, to be joined by new saloon cars for MG and Riley. Palmer was required to use standard Nuffield engines, gearboxes and rear axles but had a free hand with the styling, chassis and suspension.

Design Influences

In terms of chassis design, Palmer's own philosophy – a rigid chassis with compliant but well-located suspension – had been initially expressed in the Deroy and put into production with the Javelin. The results combined a comfortable ride with excellent road manners.

For styling, though, his influences were more wide-ranging, coming principally from Italy and the USA. The Javelin's profile followed the example of the radical 1936 Lincoln-Zephyr but fashion in the motor industry moves fast, and by the time the war ended the teardrop profile was dead in the US, chased out by more bulbous styles bedecked with heavy chrome ornamentation.

While some European car manufacturers aped American trends, others looked toward the leading European stylists, especially those from Italy. Palmer had been a disciple of Italian car design since his boyhood in Africa and the styles springing from the great design houses of Milan and Turin in the late 1940s impressed him deeply. Every European motor show would include a display of their latest concepts, usually based on a contemporary production model.

The Milan-based stylist Carrozzeria Touring Superleggera displayed a Lancia Aprilia fitted with their own four-door saloon body, incorporating a patented 'Aerlux' glass roof panel, at the Geneva and Turin motor shows in 1948. A glance at the few contemporary photos that exist leaves little doubt that this provided much of the inspiration not only

This 1947/8 Lancia Aprilia with 'Aerlux' bodywork by Touring of Milan included some clear styling cues developed by Palmer in his ZA Magnette. Note how the traditional Lancia grille has been blended into the 'airsmoothed' nose, the position of the front lights, the wing lines and of course the distinctive 'hockey stick' wing flashes. (Photo courtesy of Bianchi Anderloni Family Archives)

Another view of Touring's Lancia Aprilia showing the ingenious 'Aerlux' plexiglass semi-opening roof. (Photo courtesy of Bianchi Anderloni Family Archives)

A 1950 Alfa Romeo 6C 2500 with bodywork by Touring of Milan displaying many of the design features from the earlier Lancia Aprilia. This model is a particularly harmonious design, helped by the proportions of the underlying chassis. (Photo courtesy of National Motor Museum, Beaulieu)

A 1950 Lancia B50 Coupé with bodywork by Vignale, another example of Italian styling of the period which, even in this rather dejected condition, has the grace and elegance admired by Palmer. (Author)

for the production of the Lancia Aurelia saloon and coupé introduced from 1950, but also for Palmer's new range of cars. Touring's styling featured a streamlined version of the traditional Lancia radiator grille, blended seamlessly into the flowing lines of the nose. The front wings, set somewhat below the bonnet line, swept gracefully back in a gentle curve from the headlights. Twin fog lights enhanced the space between the headlights and the grille, while horizontal chrome features along the flanks emphasised the car's length. In a final flourish, tapering mouldings swept back from the Lancia's wheel arches. Over the next couple of years these design cues found their way onto some of Italy's most prestigious sporting brands – exotic names to which MG customers might aspire. In an era of drab austerity, they spoke of a new and exciting future.

The Design Takes Shape

Palmer planned two basic bodyshells sharing many common design and production features. The smaller four-seat saloon shell was to be used on the MG and four-cylinder Wolseley models while a larger six-seat bodyshell would bear Riley and Wolseley badges.

He tackled the MG and Riley first. A very early sketch dating from 1949 demonstrates clearly Palmer's interpretation of Touring's contemporary styling concepts. The production model lost the chrome flash to the rear wheel arch and gained its distinctive spotlights

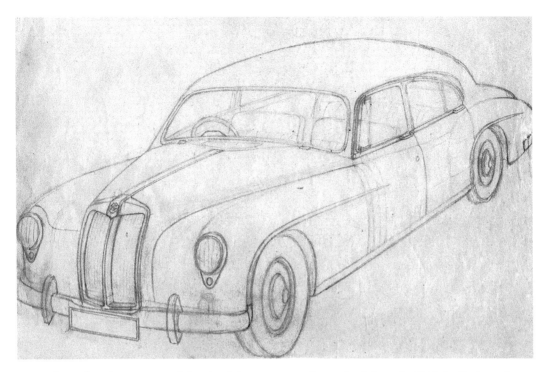

The earliest known pencil sketch of the Magnette, drawn by Palmer in 1949. It displays almost all the characteristics of the 1953 production model. (Courtesy of Celia Palmer)

but the sketch is otherwise instantly recognisable, even down to the semi-octagon of the speedometer peeking over the lower edge of the windscreen! The 1953 Riley Pathfinder also echoed Touring's Lancia Aprilia Aerlux, especially from the front.

Palmer's advocacy of intelligent suspension design was reflected in his proposals for the smaller MG and Wolseley saloons. At the front he designed a set-up comprising an upper wishbone and single lower arm, the latter braced rearwards by a substantial tie-rod attached to the body. A second tie-rod led forwards from the top wishbone. Coil springs incorporated coaxial telescopic dampers, while rack and pinion steering mounted in front of the axle line completed what was an advanced layout for a production saloon car at the time.

At the rear Palmer was limited by having to use a standard Nuffield live rear axle. In the Wolseley this was conventionally fixed to semi-elliptic leaf springs with U-bolts, though the inclined telescopic dampers were a considerable improvement over the lever-arm units fitted to lesser Nuffield products. The Magnette design blazed a more adventurous trail that was driven by the fact that the car sat 2 inches lower than the Wolseley. To prevent the propshaft from touching the tunnel as the springs were compressed, Palmer designed a Bugatti-inspired torque arm fixed to the left-hand side of the differential casing and running forward to a mounting point on the side of the propshaft tunnel. The axle itself was flexibly mounted on the rear springs. As the springs were compressed, the torque arm would twist the axle, deflecting the nose of the differential casing downwards and thus keeping the propshaft clear of the tunnel.

The 2.5-litre Riley Pathfinder launched with the Magnette in 1953 was a larger car but was clearly one of Palmer's 'family' of BMC cars. (Photo courtesy of Celia Palmer)

Italianate styling in Oxford – Palmer's house in Iffley, which he designed in the early 1950s and occupied for the rest of his life. The curved staircase behind the semicircular façade was inspired by Alfa Romeo's head office in Milan. His daughter Celia poses with the author's ZA Magnette. (Author)

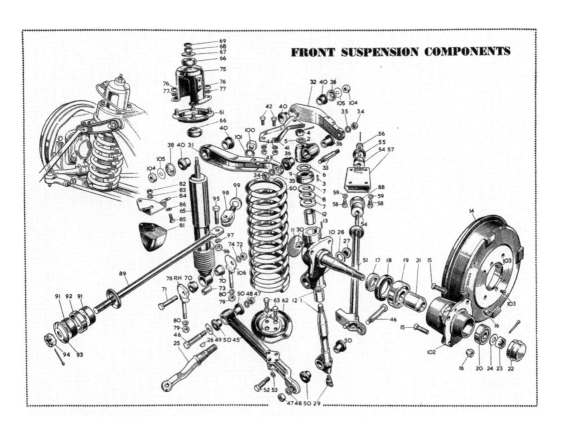

The Magnette's front suspension design was shared with the Wolseley but was never adopted elsewhere in the BMC range despite its superior qualities.

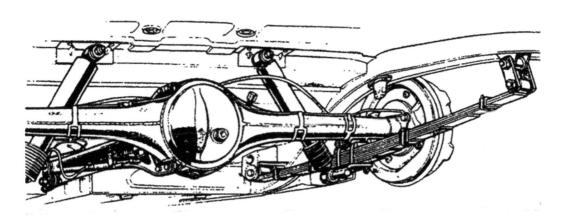

The original design for the rear suspension was unique to the Magnette but did not reach production. This drawing clearly shows the Bugatti-inspired torque arm bolted to the differential casing. (Courtesy of Magnette Register Archives)

Magnette and 4/44 – Rationalisation Goes Awry

One of the principal aims of the Nuffield directors had been to rationalise production by using common components in the MG, Wolseley and Riley ranges, with differences between the marques being achieved by more subtle variations of trim, badging and performance, an approach that later became known as 'badge engineering'. It is therefore surprising to see just how different the MG Magnette and Wolseley 4/44 were in practice. For example, of all the exterior body panels, only the roof, front doors and boot lid were interchangeable, mainly because the Magnette's ride height was 2 inches lower than the Wolseley's. At the front, the Wolseley's higher stance was achieved not, as might be expected, by fitting longer springs, but by mounting the front chassis legs in a lower position relative to the body. Rear suspension mountings were also different and, as the body was higher relative to the wheels, the position of the wheel arch in the wing was lower on the Wolseley to avoid an unsightly gap between the top of the wheels and the wheel arches. The sills also differed, with those on the Magnette rolling inwards beneath the doors while the Wolseley sills adopted the reverse profile.

As well as being lower-slung, the Magnette announced its presence with a distinctive take on the traditional MG radiator grille. This flowed into the car's curvaceous lines in the style first seen in Palmers's 1949 sketch and lifted with the bonnet. By contrast the Wolseley retained the company's distinctive and more upright grille which remained fixed when the bonnet was raised, necessitating further changes to the metalwork.

Cabin design also emphasised the cars' different characters. The Wolseley driver faced a traditional wood-veneered dashboard with a centrally mounted instrument panel and switches. A split bench front seat necessitated a column-mounted gear change and an umbrella-style handbrake lever beneath the dashboard. The Magnette was aimed at the more enthusiastic driver, so the instruments and most switches were mounted in direct line of sight behind the steering wheel. There was a centrally placed gear lever and handbrake and individual front seats held the driver and passenger more firmly in place when the driver felt inclined to exploit the car's cornering abilities.

Magnette ZA and Wolseley 4/44 head-to-head – this shows the difference in ride height between the two models and the Wolseley's consequently deeper bodywork. (Author)

The frontal view of the Magnette and 4/44 clearly emphasises the ride height and stance of each car and the features which contribute to their distinct characters. (Author)

The Engine Dilemma

In principle, rationalisation might have been easier to achieve for the new cars' engines. The new cars had to use existing production units, meaning there was a choice of three: the Riley 1½-litre (a twin-camshaft design being used in the RMA), the Wolseley 1½-litre employed in the 4/50 saloon and the 1¼-litre engine from the MG Y-type saloon, also used in modified form in the TD Midget sports car. However, none really fitted the bill. Despite being the most powerful (55 bhp), the Riley engine had its origins in the 1920s and was so steeped in Riley tradition that it was deemed inappropriate for MG use. The Wolseley engine was of relatively advanced overhead camshaft design but developed a rather pedestrian 51 bhp, while the MG engine produced 46 bhp in the Y-type saloon and 54 bhp in the Midget and dated back to 1938.

But change was afoot. In November 1951 an agreement was reached for the merger of the Nuffield Group with its great UK rival the Austin Motor Company to create the British Motor Corporation (BMC). The merger was completed in March 1952 and BMC became the largest UK motor manufacturer, with nearly 40 per cent of the total British market.

The merger offered the option of a new and more powerful 1½-litre engine, the new BMC B-series, which had been developed by Austin. This was a conventional cast-iron four-cylinder design with overhead valves operated via pushrods and rockers. Though not adventurous in engineering terms, it was a sturdy unit with the potential for tuning and enlargement, and went on to have a long and successful production life, ending in 1980 with the demise of the MGB.

With the potential for more than 60 bhp, such modern engineering was an obvious choice for the new MG, but the engine was not ready for production in time for the planned launch at the 1952 London Motor Show. The decision was therefore made to launch the Wolseley in 1952, equipped with the old MG Y-type 1¼-litre engine, and to delay the launch of the MG until the following year.

The Prototypes

The first Magnette prototype was produced by Pressed Steel, BMC's Cowley body plant, in early 1953. It carried chassis number KAK13/EX215. As may be seen from Appendix 3, the first three letters indicated this was a Magnette with a four-door saloon body and finished in light red. The first two numbers identify it as having right-hand drive and a cellulose paint finish. The second part of the number shows that this was a prototype; EX letters were used by MG and Morris for all experimental projects. This car was registered UFC 476. The second prototype, KAE13/EX216, was manufactured in July 1953 and was registered UFC 764.

Testing by the Experimental Department in Cowley appears to have gone well until the early autumn when two of the testers, Joe Gomm and Peter Tothill, were overtaking another vehicle at around 75 mph on the A40 Witney Road to the north-west of Oxford. A car coming in the opposite direction pulled out without warning, forcing the driver, Gomm, to brake heavily. More than forty years later, Tothill vividly recalled what happened next[1]: 'It was terrifying – the car developed violent axle tramp which built up and up. It became quite uncontrollable and we were all over the road.' Luckily the car eventually slewed to a halt without hitting anything but it was driven straight back to Cowley, one assumes with a degree of caution, so that the problem could be investigated.

Palmer was initially sceptical until he found he could readily reproduce the behaviour on the test track. The problem lay in his novel rear suspension design which caused the axle to twist and release rapidly when braking heavily from high speed. With the Earl's Court Motor show due to start on 21 October there was no time to engineer a solution; instead, the rear suspension had to revert to the traditional design found on the Wolseley, with the axle bolted directly to the springs. To overcome the problem of the propshaft contacting the tunnel, the bump-stops were modified to limit the upward travel of the axle and different springs with a greater camber were specified, resulting in the characteristic slight 'tail up' stance of the production cars.

With last-minute modifications completed, the Magnette was, in the nick of time, ready to meet the public.

1. Interview with author, 1996.

UFC 476, the first Magnette prototype, pictured in the summer of 1953. It lacks the front bumper overriders and spotlights that featured on all production models, the wheels are body-coloured and the front door windows are without the quarterlights that were fitted after the first 250 cars had been produced. (Photo courtesy of National Motor Museum, Beaulieu)

5

The Magnette
Meets the Market

The Launch

The press launch of the new MG Magnette took place on Friday 16 October 1953 in Nuffield House, Piccadilly in the West End of London. Two other new models took to the stage with the Magnette: the Riley Pathfinder and the MG TF Midget. The date was chosen to coincide with the Motor Show edition of *The Autocar*, arguably Britain's premier motoring magazine, and the car was chassis number 502, the second production car, which was finished in metallic Twilight Grey with light-grey interior trim.

Five days later the public had the chance to see the new models for themselves at the London Motor Show at Earl's Court. There were two Magnettes on display: chassis number 501 (the first production car) was finished in metallic MG Green with biscuit-coloured interior trim, while 503 was in metallic Twilight Grey with matching trim.

The new car was marketed under the slogan 'Safety Fast – in airsmoothed style'. MG adopted the 'Safety Fast' slogan in the 1930s and used it consistently for decades – indeed, it is still the name of the MG Car Club's monthly magazine. 'Airsmoothed', though, was new and emphasised the radical breakaway in styling from the classic pre-war perpendicular to the new era of streamlining.

Pricing reflected the Magnette's market position. The ex-factory price was £645 plus 42 per cent purchase tax in the UK, bringing the total to £915. This was just £10 more than the Magnette's predecessor, the 1¼-litre Y-type and £61 more than the Wolseley 4/44. BMC's more prosaic models of a similar size, the Morris Oxford and Austin Cambridge, were some £200 less.

Initially the Magnette was offered in just four exterior colours: metallic Twilight Grey, metallic MG Green, Autumn Red and Black.

The Autocar devoted three pages to the Magnette in a piece that included a detailed technical description and a cutaway drawing of the car. The press had not been offered a chance to drive the new model and the haste with which the cars had been prepared for the launch is clear. The article refers to a number of pre-production details that were not seen in production models, most notably the original rear suspension design, suggesting that a final resolution of the problem discovered during tests might not have been completed in time for the Motor Show.

The press launch in Nuffield House, London, on 16 October 1953. Gerald Palmer addresses the delegates with the second production car, chassis number 502, on display. (Photo courtesy of Celia Palmer)

Public Reaction

The new Magnette aroused some strong opinions among the motoring public, expressed in letters to the motoring press. Its contemporary, svelte lines were the subject of praise: in a letter to *The Motor* on 15 September 1954, D. Alton considered 'the MG ZA Magnette saloon to be the best-looking production car in the world at a price of under four figures and it has a performance which is quite remarkable', sentiments that were echoed by a letter from C. T. Sanders who commented, in relation to the Magnette: 'Beautiful cars have clean, functional lines, free from contrasting angles and superfluous ornamentation. '

On the other hand, some MG traditionalists were horrified that the Magnette name, famously associated with the legendary supercharged six-cylinder K3 Magnette of the mid-1930s, had been applied to a saloon car that looked quite unlike any previous MG, had an Austin engine and, perhaps worst of all, was clearly a close cousin of the (MG-engined!) Wolseley. Writing in the December 1953 issue of *Motor Sport*, Gustaf Giers from Stockholm suggested it was 'an insult to the memory of the late Cecil Kimber to call this announced vehicle a Magnette'. This generated several months of heated debate in the magazine, though in the March 1954 edition, John Noble of Oxford correctly pointed out that many pre-war Magnettes had been four-seater saloons with a more modest performance.

The First Road Tests

Given the volume of highly charged, subjective opinion that was being generated, BMC's delay in releasing cars for objective appraisal by the motoring journals seems odd. The first UK road test was actually published in *Autosport* on 30 July 1954, when the editor, Gregor Grant, achieved a 'scoop' by the simple expedient of testing his personal car, an early non-quarterlight model registered 414 BMD.

The report was highly complimentary. The engine was described as 'one of the sweetest four-cylinder units we have come across' and the gearbox received high praise. Grant also liked the level of standard equipment, which included such rare items as a heater/demister, windscreen washers and a dipping rear view mirror and agreed with the public's opinion of the styling, saying 'many people go so far as to say that the Magnette is the prettiest British car on the market'. He concluded the Magnette was 'an ideal fast tourer' but looked forward to the time when a more powerful version might be available. Grant was an enthusiastic rally driver and competed in his car on the Monte Carlo Rally in 1955 – with disastrous results. However, the car was repaired and Grant used it to compete in the 1956 Mille Miglia race in Italy and as a tow car for his Lotus Eleven for the same event in 1957.

A press car was finally released to Britain's pre-eminent weekly motor magazines, *The Autocar* and *The Motor,* in late 1954, more than a year after the launch. This was a black car, registered KBL 285. *The Autocar*'s report appeared first, on 26 November 1954, and was fulsome in its praise even by the standards of the day, when a more deferential generation of journalists cloaked their criticisms in the subtlest of language. The testers commented on the extremely high standards of roadholding and handling, and managed to negotiate a bend on a private test circuit, in the rain, faster than any car previously tested in wet or dry conditions. Performance, comfort and equipment were also admired, with small gripes reserved only for the position of some of the switches and a draught beneath the dashboard. In summary, the test report concluded '...the MG Magnette is one of the finer cars *The Autocar* has tested. It is extremely comfortable, good looking and safe'.

The subject of the first road test, Gregor Grant's early ZA registered 414 BMD, led a hard life. Competing in the 1955 Monte Carlo Rally, it encountered a tree near Grenoble. (Photo courtesy of National Motor Museum, Beaulieu)

The Motor, whose road test appeared on 5 January 1955, had a few more criticisms. It also picked up on the switch layout and the under-dashboard draught (perhaps a fault on that particular car), and subtly criticised the final drive gearing, suggesting 'the axle ratio chosen favours acceleration rather than maximum speed'. The ride, especially in the rear seats, was thought to be rather too firm and the demisting arrangements were 'none too effective'. In conclusion, though, the magazine pronounced that 'the MG Magnette proves itself a very good example indeed of an extremely British type of car ... It is a car we have found extremely pleasant to drive on British roads, and which should also prove well suited to requirements in many other parts of the world.'

The mid-1950s saw a continuation of the 'export or die' policy that had governed Britain's economic agenda since the end of the war, so overseas markets were an important target. By this time the MG marque was firmly established in the USA, helped by returning former GIs who had developed a taste for small sports cars during their European postings. The curiously named magazine *Air Trials Hobbies for Young Men* was well ahead of the UK with its road test of the Magnette in July 1954, while the respected *Road and Track* profiled the car in its December edition. In a market more used to V8-engined behemoths, it concluded that 'for a car with individuality, good driving traits and a "custom" quality, the Magnette just about fits the bill'. The Australian *Modern Motor* magazine profiled the 'New MG Saloon' prior to its appearance at the 1954 Sydney Motor Show, though this was before cars had arrived in the country so no road test was possible.

The Magnette had taken a surprisingly long time to come to the market and even longer to receive a stamp of approval from the motoring press. Production had been very slow to start with, but by the end of 1954 3,823 cars had been produced and the car was beginning to make its mark.

The second-oldest Magnette known to exist, chassis No. 528, built December 1953 to February 1954. This was the 1954 Copenhagen Motor Show car, and was discovered in a Danish field in the 1980s. Poul Dalkov completed a meticulous restoration in 2015, carefully retaining the features unique to the very early cars. The colour is Autumn Red. (Photo courtesy of Poul Dalkov)

6

Growing Up and Growing Old – Production Changes 1954–58

Early Production

Production problems probably explain the 'soft launch' of the Magnette. No press cars were available and sales did not begin until February 1954. Even then, the supply was no more than a trickle. Production records indicate that the build time of the first twenty cars, commenced between October and December 1953, averaged between two and three months per car. It is believed most of these cars were fitted with the original rear suspension, which had to be modified, and a significant number were destined for motor shows around the world. Series production is thought to have started in February 1954, at around chassis number 580, which took two weeks to build. Number 592 was completed in ten days and by 641 the standard period of production was one week.

Apart from the rear suspension, a number of other more minor differences identified the first 250 production cars. Most obvious was the lack of front quarterlights, while rear light plinths on these early cars were in rubber and the lights themselves were slightly smaller in diameter. The radiator grille had two shorter outer slats and a slightly different profile to the surround.

After its rushed launch and the subsequent slow start to full-scale production, the ZA Magnette was then subject to a number of more minor changes during 1954. Opening quarterlights were fitted to the front doors from chassis number 750 and from around number 1,860 a bypass pipe was installed between the oil filter and the rear of the engine block to improve circulation. Probably reflecting what was available in the parts bin at the time, the fuel filler flap gained key operation from 2,127, but it seems that particular bin ran out in mid-1955, when push-button operation was reintroduced! From 2,632 the rear light plinths were altered and larger-diameter lights were fitted. Finally, for the 1954 London Motor Show, the metallic MG Green and Twilight Grey colours were dropped and replaced by non-metallic versions of the same shades.

The first 250 production cars differed in many ways from later examples. This picture illustrates the smaller rear lights fitted to No. 528, the Danish Motor Show car. (Photo courtesy of Poul Dalkov)

Another picture of No. 528 shows how part of Palmer's aborted torque arm was retained in truncated form on the very early cars and used as a mounting bracket for the handbrake balancing link. (Photo courtesy of Poul Dalkov)

An interior shot of an early ZA showing the original composite metal/wood dashboard fitted up to car No. 6501. (Photo courtesy of Anthony White)

The later all-wood ZA dashboard showing the revised switchgear layout and the central ashtray. (Photo courtesy of Grant Howlett)

Gerald Palmer poses in front of a fine example of a 1955 ZA Magnette owned by Andrew Brock in 1997. This car represents the specification for the ZA finally established after more than a year of small changes. (Photo courtesy of Andrew Brock)

In spring 1955, from number 6,501 the original dashboard, which was finished in a mix of genuine wood veneer and metal painted to match the wood, was replaced by an all-wood version finished in an attractive combination of straight-grained and burr walnut veneer. Perhaps in response to the road testers' comments, the new dash incorporated revisions to the switch layout, while the ashtrays at either end were replaced with a single, centrally mounted item. At number 8,072, some subtle changes were made to the radiator grille.

Later ZA Changes

The only change of note for the 1956 model year was a revised range of colours, introduced between July and September 1955. Black and Twilight Grey options were continued but MG Green was dropped in favour of the lighter Island Green. Autumn Red was replaced by the subtly different shade of Damask Red and three new colours were introduced: Steel Blue, Birch Grey and Royal Tan, the last a rather odd shade of beige/brown. Royal Tan was only available for August and September 1955, presumably being killed off by resistance from the dealers – which, in the author's opinion, was well-founded!

The engine compartment of Grant Howlett's ZA is standard with the exception of the electric windscreen washer pump supplementing the original vacuum-driven system and the finish to the carburettors – the factory never achieved such a shine! (Photo courtesy of Grant Howlett)

More significant changes were made to the ZA in mid-1956, with the aim of improving performance and high-speed cruising. By 1956 the 1,489cc B-series engine had found its way into a number of BMC vehicles, most notably the new MGA sports car which had been announced in autumn 1955. In the MGA the engine initially had an output of 68 bhp at 5,500 rpm (by comparison with the Magnette's 60 bhp at 4,600 rpm) which was achieved through the fitting of larger SU carburettors (1½ inch instead of 1¼ inch), a higher compression ratio (8.3:1 compared with 7.15:1) and a better-designed exhaust manifold. Installing this engine in the Magnette was straightforward and, with more power, the car could take a higher rear axle ratio, leading to more relaxed high-speed travel without a loss of acceleration or hill-climbing ability.

In early 1956 MG produced a small number of cars to this specification for appraisal. One of these ended up in the hands of Geoff Duke, who had won two 350cc world motorcycle championships with Norton in 1951 and 1952, followed by world 500cc championships with Gilera in 1953, 1954 and 1955 – excellent publicity for MG, who doubtless judged Duke to be the sort of chap who could handle that extra 8 bhp!

The uprated engine, linked to the higher ratio (4.55:1) rear axle, was fitted to production ZA Magnettes from June 1956, starting with chassis number 18101. There was no publicity fanfare and the only visual changes under the bonnet were the new, larger carburettors fed via a revised cast alloy manifold and air filter. Externally, the eagle-eyed enthusiast may just have spotted that the four jacking points originally mounted on the front and rear bumper irons had been replaced by a pair of jacking points mounted under the sills on either side of the car.

The ZB Magnette

At the 1956 London Motor Show just four months later, the ZB Magnette replaced the ZA. In effect, therefore, the more powerful late ZA was a short-run prototype of the ZB, with just 476 being produced.

The ZB had the 68 bhp engine and 4.55:1 axle and also featured some subtle cosmetic changes. The distinctive curved 'hockey stick' chrome flashes on the front wings inspired by Touring's late 1940s designs were replaced by a simple straight chrome strip mounted above the front wheel arches and running back halfway across the front doors. Internally there was a new dished steering wheel with a different spoke configuration and a change to the lower part of the dashboard behind the wheel allowing a further rearrangement of some of the switches. The gear lever acquired a revised oval rubber boot and associated chrome trim to allow for the different position of the Manumatic gear lever, described later, while a useful parcel shelf appeared below the dashboard, replacing the ZA's single map pocket.

Minor tweaks indeed, but also announced at the same time was the ZB Varitone, a new Magnette variant with a little more glitz. Mechanically identical to the standard ZB, the clue to the new model was in the name – it was available in a range of two-colour combinations, and was a bold attempt to keep pace with the fashions of the time as the drab post-war period began to edge towards the swinging sixties. Colour combinations ranged from the subtle Birch Grey/Twilight Grey to the decidedly eye-catching Island/Sage Green and Ivory/Maroon options. In all cases the darker colours were on the lower half of

A quarter-scale model of the ZB Magnette produced in the Cowley factory, probably in early 1956. The only obvious external difference from the ZA is the replacement of the 'hockey stick' front wing trim with a straight, tapering chrome strip. (Photo courtesy of the MG Car Club)

A ZB engine bay showing the larger 1½-inch carburettors, the new inlet manifold and air cleaner. The control box and fuses were mounted in a different position on the bulkhead, which meant the chassis plate was moved to the top face of the bulkhead. This car has a non-standard electric washer pump and bottle, the fuel filter is an addition and the battery is smaller than the original. (Photo courtesy of Alan Cleobury)

The ZB dashboard showing yet another rearrangement of the switches, the dished wheel with rearranged spokes and the new parcel shelf beneath the dash. The MG gear knob and of course the seatbelts are non-standard. This car is a Varitone but the standard ZB interior was identical. (Photo courtesy of Alan Cleobury)

the body with lighter shades above, separated by a narrow chrome strip running from the top of the radiator grille to the scuttle, and thence along the swage line on the doors and rear wing moulding, down to the rear lights. The standard ZB's front wing strips did not feature on the Varitone.

The second obvious feature was the Varitone's much larger rear window, which curved across the whole of the rear of the cabin, providing a much airier feel for the rear seat passengers. In production terms, this was something of an afterthought, and for the whole of the production run Pressed Steel only produced bodyshells with small rear windows. The aperture for the Varitone's larger window was cut out by hand, one-by-one as required, at the Morris Motors body shop.

By 1956 trafficators were looking decidedly old-hat and all Varitones were equipped with flashing indicators showing a white light within the front sidelights and red from the rear tail/brake light units. Standard ZBs destined for most export markets also had flashing indicators but in the UK this was an optional extra.

For those who did not fancy the newfangled two-tone paintwork but wanted the other benefits offered by the Varitone, a single colour option was available by special order. All-over black or maroon cars seem to have been most popular but the managing director of MG, John Thornley, pulled rank and arranged for his car, chassis number 23358, to be painted in overall metallic Twilight Grey, a colour that had only been available to the public in the first year of Magnette production.

The 1956 Motor Show edition of *Autosport* magazine featured a full-page colour advertisement of the MG range with the new ZB Varitone in pride of place. (Photo courtesy of MGCC Magnette Register Records)

Peter Martin's 1958 ZB in Kashmir Beige/Wolseley Maroon shortly after its restoration in 1999. Peter has since covered over 130,000 miles in the car! The amber front indicators are non-standard. Other Varitone colour combinations in the picture are Birch Grey/Twilight Grey and Steel Blue/Black. (Photo courtesy of Peter Martin)

The Varitone colours and larger rear screen make a big difference to the Magnette's appearance from the rear. This 1957 standard ZB in Island Green and 1958 ZB Varitone in Ivory/Black are both owned by David Halliday. (Photo courtesy of David Halliday)

The new ZB Magnette was slightly more expensive than its predecessor at £693 basic, or £1,041 with UK Purchase Tax. For the Varitone buyers paid £718 (£1,078 with tax), but prices rose further within a few months. From 1957 until the end of production they were £714 (£1,072) and £740 (£1,111) respectively. This made the Magnette more expensive than its nearest British rival, Rootes' Sunbeam Rapier, a two-door sports saloon with American-influenced styling introduced in 1955. The Rapier had an engine of 1,390cc developing 62 bhp (67.5 bhp from October 1956) and cost £695 (£1,043).

At the same time as the ZB was launched, the Wolseley 4/44 was replaced by the very similar-looking Wolseley 15/50. The MG-origin 1250cc engine of the 4/44 was replaced by the 1,489cc B-series engine – essentially a single carburettor version of the engine fitted to the ZB Magnette.

The Manumatic Gearbox

The Magnette had from the start been a very well-equipped car and the factory options list had been limited to a rather expensive radio, costing nearly £45. However, from the start of ZB production, and for an extra £50 (including Purchase Tax), a buyer could specify a 'Manumatic' gearbox which, as the name suggests, was a halfway house between a manual and a fully automatic means of gear selection.

A Manumatic-equipped car had no clutch pedal but retained a conventional gear lever which selected the four forward speeds and reverse in the usual H pattern. To get going, the driver started the engine and (without a clutch to depress) engaged first gear. Pressing the accelerator progressively then engaged a centrifugal clutch and the car began to move. To change gear, the driver grasped the gear lever and moved it to the new position, but this simple action generated a flurry of electro-mechanical activity. The gear lever knob incorporated a microswitch which operated a pair of solenoids and servos in the control unit. These opened or closed the accelerator at the carburettor, independently of the accelerator pedal's position, and also disengaged and re-engaged the clutch via a synchroniser switch on the clutch cover which matched the engine speed to that of the clutch-driven plate. A valve incorporated in the control unit ensured progressive engagement of the clutch. To stop, the driver simply used the footbrake; the centrifugal clutch would disengage when engine revs fell to idling speed.

Automatic transmission was becoming increasingly popular in the USA but in the mid-1950s the gearboxes available were relatively heavy and cumbersome and thus not suitable for smaller cars. The Manumatic gearbox was introduced with one eye on the USA market, but it was not a success. For a start, driving a Manumatic car took some getting used to. In particular, clutch engagement was very sensitive to the engine's idling speed. This could lead to unexpected forward or backward movement of the car if the revs were higher than usual – for example, if the engine was cold and the choke lever had been pulled out. There could also be a fairly sharp take-off from rest, which could make manoeuvring in a confined space a somewhat exciting procedure.

The Manumatic gearbox also turned out to be exceptionally unreliable, and a glance at the workshop manual suggests why. Three pneumatic servos, two pneumatic solenoids, three electrical switches, one hydraulic and one pneumatic valve all had to perform

DIAGRAM ILLUSTRATING A TYPICAL
Manumatic TRANSMISSION SYSTEM
WITH HYDRAULIC CLUTCH-OPERATING LINKAGE

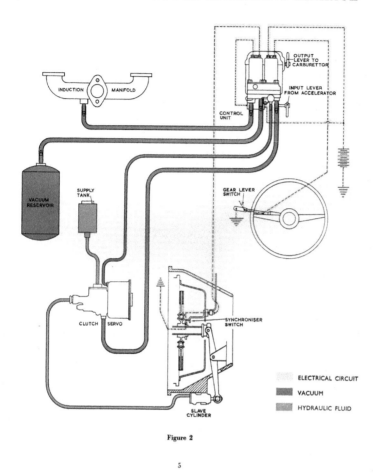

Figure 2

A diagram showing the basic components of the Manumatic transmission system. This illustrates a column-mounted gear lever, but the principles of operation for a floor-mounted lever are identical. (Photo courtesy of MGCC Magnette Register Records)

faultlessly every time a gear change was required. A fault in any component would lead to failure and diagnosis was tricky, to say the least. For the average garage mechanic this was black magic, and the workshop manual, which took nine pages to describe how the system worked and a further thirty-four covering maintenance and fault-finding, did little to put his mind at rest.

A great idea, then, but one which was ahead of its day, and well in advance of the technology that would have been needed to make it reliable. Only 496 Manumatic Magnettes were produced, of which 246 were sold to the home market; the majority of the remainder went to North America. Many are believed to have been converted back to a conventional gearbox (a service offered by dealerships for a mere £75 – on top of the original £50 option price!) and none is known to be in a roadworthy condition today.

ZB Road Tests

By 1956 the Magnette was a well-established model and was becoming much respected among the cognoscenti. Press comments were generally highly favourable. In the UK, *The Autocar* followed its very complimentary review of the ZA in January 1955 with high praise for the ZB in its 5 July 1957 edition. The car tested was a Twilight Grey standard ZB registered MBL 665, which the tester wound up to 86.5 mph (their ZA had managed 80.7 mph), making the car 'our fastest native 1½ litre four-door saloon'. Handling, brakes and gear change were highly regarded and the testers praised the interior space and fit-out. *The Motor*'s test of the same car appeared on 21 August 1957 and began by noting the significant performance improvements over the ZA, going on to revel in the delights of the leather upholstery, the fine veneered finish to the dash and door cappings and the high level of standard equipment. The Magnette was 'a car designed for long distance travel in the hands of a determined driver' though the magazine did still consider the gearing to be too low and commented that interior noise level in the 60–75 mph band 'does tarnish the pleasure of high-speed cruising'. In summarising their opinions, though, *The Motor* concluded 'the ZB Magnette can be accounted one of the most charming and attractive small cars that has come into our hands. The true nature of the vehicle goes beyond the confines of the figures reported ... and indeed beyond the power of words readily available in the text.'

Almost the last word came in John Bolster's test published in *Autosport* on 20 June 1958, only six months before production ceased. Bolster concluded the ZB Magnette was 'the best (car) in the BMC range' – praise indeed!

The Magnette's appeal continued to spread beyond the UK. The US 'Small Car Guide' for 1958 was fulsome in its praise, describing the ZB Magnette as 'one of the most beautiful cars coming to the US'. Though performance was 'not sensational', it was found to be 'a highly roadable car'.

The ZB in Production

While the ZA Magnette was subject to numerous small changes over the first eighteen months of production, during just over two years of ZB manufacture the model remained essentially unaltered. Child safety locks were added to the rear doors in late 1957 and the headlining was changed from wool to plastic in early 1958, the only other change being two revised colour options offered on Varitone models at around the same time (Kashmir Beige over Wolseley Maroon and Island Green over Dark Green).

Sales remained strong: 7,365 ZAs and ZBs were produced in 1956, while for 1957 and 1958 ZB production figures were 6,996 and 9,464 respectively.

Given its continuing popularity, it is perhaps surprising that BMC decided to cease production of the ZB Magnette in late 1958. Manufacture of the final car, chassis number 37101, was started on 20 December 1958 and this car, plus twenty-six others, was completed in January 1959.

But things were changing at BMC. The ZA Magnette and its cousin the Wolseley 4/44 had been among the first examples of the policy of rationalisation following the 1951 merger of Austin and Morris, and this process was continuing. For 1959 a new range of mid-sized saloon cars was planned, offering Morris, Austin, Wolseley, MG and Riley versions of essentially the same car. The body design, used on the virtually identical Austin Cambridge and Morris Oxford, was by the Italian styling house of Pinin Farina and was very much in the contemporary American mode, featuring high tail fins and extensive use of chrome. The more upmarket models, the Wolseley 15/60, MG Magnette Mk III and Riley 4/68, featured a traditional marque radiator grille blended into the basic Farina design and some additional exterior and interior trim variations styled in-house at Longbridge. But beneath the contemporary glitz lay a shared and distinctly unsporting chassis design of Austin origin and the now familiar 1500cc B-series engine, mildly uprated to ZB specification in the MG and Riley models.

Marque individuality was finally sacrificed at the altar of pragmatic production economics and what had been arguably BMC's finest saloon car, the Z-series MG Magnette, was finished.

An artist's impression of the 1959 MG Magnette Mk III taken from the launch brochure. The Mk III was a roomy, comfortable vehicle but in the four-word tagline only the word 'car' was strictly accurate! (Photo courtesy of MGCC Magnette Register Records)

7

Improving the Breed

It took time but in the end the press, the public and even dyed-in-the-wool MG enthusiasts came to realise that the MG Magnette was an exceedingly good car in its own right and was by no means just a badge-engineered Wolseley. However, it was not perfect; reference has already been made to press reports which highlighted its relatively modest performance and low gearing. The ZB Magnette made modest attempts to tackle these issues but the quality of the chassis meant that the car was capable of handling much greater power, if only it could be provided.

The Magnette Six

The obvious answer was a larger engine and in 1956 the Engineering Development Department of the MG factory in Abingdon set about creating a six-cylinder version of the Magnette, no doubt with an eye on the stylish 2.4-litre six-cylinder Jaguar Mk 1 saloon, launched in 1955.

Though the Abingdon plant was an offshoot of the mighty BMC empire, its general manager, John Thornley, was not someone who toed the corporate line too rigorously. The Development Department under Alec Hounslow was the scene for many projects that were not, it seems, always strictly sanctioned by the chiefs in Longbridge or Cowley. It was this atmosphere of unofficial innovation and experiment that spawned the creation of the six-cylinder Magnette.

A new 2.6-litre straight-six engine, the BMC C-series, had first appeared in 1954, powering Austin's A90 Westminster saloon. Though only producing 85 bhp in the Austin, this was a smooth, modern unit with much potential – tuned versions produced 117 bhp in the Austin Healey 100/6 of 1956 and 150 bhp in the Austin-Healey 3000. In his office in Abingdon one can imagine Thornley putting two and two together, and thus it was that EX202 (the experimental code for the new model) was conceived.

A 1955 Austin A90 Westminster – the donor car for the experimental six-cylinder Magnette. (Photo courtesy of Robin Lawton)

The C-series 2.6-litre six-cylinder engine developed 85 bhp in the Westminster but could be tuned to produce much more. (Photo courtesy of Robin Lawton)

Sadly, no photos or drawings remain of this intriguing vehicle but Don Hayter, who arrived in Abingdon from Aston Martin in February 1956 as a body engineer, recalls that 'the car was a knife-and-fork job, based on a standard car off the line that was then cut and modified to fit the Austin engine'.[1]

1. Interview with the author in 2006 for an article published in the MGCC magazine *Safety Fast!* in January 2007.

Fitting the long and heavy six-cylinder engine in place of the Magnette's compact four would have involved some major surgery and, despite the lack of drawings, there are clues as to how this was done. The work was carried out under the supervision of Dennis Williams, who was then Abingdon's Chief Engineer. According to Peter Neal[2], who began working in the design office at Abingdon in 1954, a standard car was mounted on a large cast-iron plate used as a form of jig and, once in place, the car was cut at the bulkhead and a new front frame installed to take the bigger engine, suspension and other ancillaries.

Both Williams and Neal recalled this frame came pretty much complete from the Westminster and Geoff Hey (No. 2 to John Thornley at the time) confirmed that the car had Austin cam and peg steering.[3] Mounting the Westminster engine and gearbox in a frame already designed for them was presumably not much of a problem, and as this was an experiment not aimed at production, expediency would have probably triumphed over any lingering concerns about an unnatural liaison between Abingdon and Longbridge.

The state of tune of the actual engine installed is unclear. Peter Neal and Dennis Williams recalled it as being pretty much the 'cooking' Austin unit, though Williams thought the standard Solex might have been replaced by twin SUs. Geoff Hey, on the other hand, suggested it may have been a tuned engine from a production car racer.[4]

To accommodate the physically much larger engine, bespoke bodywork was required. The design was the responsibility of Jim O'Neill, who had worked for Gerald Palmer as Chief Body Engineer. A longer bonnet and extended front wings were needed, and Abingdon records refer to a longer steering column (EX203). A larger radiator was necessary for the six-cylinder engine, which in turn required a bigger grille that has been described as being wider that the standard item, but retaining the characteristic Magnette swept-back curve.

Aft of the bulkhead, it seems that the six-cylinder car had unmodified Magnette bodywork but a C-type rear axle was fitted, probably also from the Westminster. Those who saw it describe the car as looking basically standard to the casual observer, with the obvious exception of the radiator grille.

By late summer of 1956 the project was complete and ready to take to the road in a smart new coat of black paint. Judging by the reactions of those who drove it, it seems the conversion was successful. Dennis Williams probably spent more time behind the wheel than anyone else, using the car for trips to Birmingham and Coventry and to visit Earls Court for the 1956 Motor Show. 'The car went extremely well, it was a car I very much enjoyed driving' he recalled, 'and it handled very well too'.[5]

Those who were allowed behind the wheel were tempted to have some fun with unsuspecting motorists. Don Hayter remembers outpacing a Jaguar, which must have been particularly satisfying, given that Jaguar would have been the main competition had the car ever reached production.

So why did a car that apparently had much potential go no further? Perhaps this was because the six-cylinder Magnette was essentially a one-off special produced by Abingdon,

2. Ibid.
3. Ibid.
4. Ibid.
5. Ibid.

lacking sanction from BMC's directors. The route from prototype to production is a long one and by late 1956 BMC was already planning the Magnette's replacement. In the interim, the market gap for a big six-cylinder high-performance saloon was filled by the Riley 2.6 in 1957, though that turned out to be something of a flop, with fewer than 1,000 being sold.

And what became of EX202? Along with most other one-off experiments it is believed to have been cut up behind the factory sometime in the late 1950s. A sad end to an intriguing experiment.

A Twin-cam Magnette?

The BMC B-series engine has many merits, among them simplicity, reliability, longevity and an ability to be tuned to produce levels of power well in excess of production standards. But as a heavy, cast-iron lump with pushrod-operated valves, it has a rugged rather than exotic character, well-suited to powering many types of road car but lacking the glamour of the twin overhead cam engines used by the likes of Alfa Romeo and Jaguar, with whom MG aspired to compete.

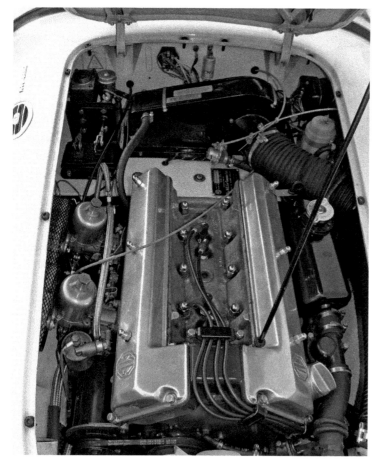

The BMC B-series twin-cam engine, fitted in an MGA Twin-Cam sports car. Its use in the Magnette was proposed but overruled. (Photo courtesy of Colin Manley)

BMC had toyed with the concept of this type of engine during the 1950s. Immediately prior to the launch of the MGA in the autumn of 1955, three prototypes were entered for the Ulster Tourist Trophy race, two of which were fitted with different designs of experimental twin overhead camshaft engines. One engine was completely new, while the other comprised a new aluminium cylinder head incorporating the camshafts but fitted to a modified BMC B-series engine block. The latter design was initiated by Gerald Palmer before his departure from BMC in September 1955 and it went on to power the EX179 record-breaker to more than 170 mph and sixteen international records at Utah in August 1956.

In the light of this success, and with a desire for a higher performance version of the MGA, the B-series twin-cam engine was prepared for production and the MGA Twin-Cam was launched in July 1958. The new engine had a power output of 108 bhp – a 50 per cent increase over the standard car's 72 bhp.

Though the cylinder head was much wider than that of the pushrod engine, fitting a twin-cam engine into the Magnette would have been a much easier operation than installing the six-cylinder C-series. It would have transformed the performance and character of the car and Marcus Chambers, who managed Abingdon's competitions department from 1955 to 1962, wanted MG to build a short run of at least 500 twin-cam Magnettes for homologation purposes in order to create a competitive works rally car. Alas, Chambers' proposal fell on deaf ears at BMC and, while it seems likely that the twin-cam engine was fitted to at least one car by way of experiment, no further progress was made.

The Pillarless Magnette

Gerald Palmer is reported to have been no fan of the body and trim changes that were introduced with the ZB Magnette, which detracted, in his opinion, from the purity of the original design. He was, however, responsible for a little-known one-off curiosity – a pillarless version of the standard Magnette bodyshell. Little is known of this car and no pictures are believed to exist so details are sketchy, but a fully functioning car was apparently built. Even more surprisingly, instead of being cut up by the factory as was the fate of almost all experimental models, it was sold to Cowley's chief development engineer, Charles Griffin, who used it as family transport for a number of years.

Pillarless bodywork, which eliminates the central 'B-post' between the front and rear windows, creates a lighter and airier feel to a saloon car, especially when all the side windows are down. The design had become popular in the USA from the mid-1950s and was featured on the Magnette's main British rival, the two-door Sunbeam Rapier. It is not known whether the pillarless Magnette had two or four doors, though from an engineering point of view two would have been much more practical and would have also suited the more sporting nature of this style of bodywork.

The experimental car was finished in two-tone cream and blue but sadly it was written off in an accident in around 1960. MG's answer to demands for a Magnette reflecting current fashion was instead the Varitone, which was no doubt much cheaper to produce but lacked that extra pizzazz of the stillborn pillarless experiment.

Modifications and Accessories

While the Abingdon factory's ideas for improving and developing the Magnette ultimately came to naught, the after-sales manufacturers grasped the opportunity of providing enthusiastic owners with ways of enhancing the performance of their cars.

The 1950s saw the emergence of an active after-sales industry devoted to performance add-ons, often developed and endorsed by the prominent racing and rally drivers of the day. These products were often genuine attempts by experienced engineers to give enthusiastic owners, who might use their cars as daily transport during the week and for amateur motor sport at weekends, a performance edge over the competition. With its sporting pretensions, the Magnette was exactly the type of car to attract the attention of such manufacturers.

Edgar de Normanville was a gifted engineer and motoring journalist who had joined the editorial staff of *The Motor* in 1908. After the First World War he became motoring correspondent for the *Daily Express* and *The Chronicle,* while continuing his calling as an innovative engineer. In the 1930s he designed an epicyclic overdrive for cars which was subsequently put into production by the Laycock Engineering Company of Sheffield.

An overdrive is a secondary gearbox fitted to the rear of a conventional car gearbox and engaged via a mechanical lever or an electric switch. It provides an additional gear ratio, lowering the rate at which the engine is revving by comparison with 'normal' (non-overdrive) top gear, thus providing quieter and more economical cruising. It may also be designed to operate when lower gears are engaged.

An early MGB gearbox, which is similar to the Magnette's unit, fitted with Laycock de Normanville overdrive. The overdrive unit itself is on the left, beneath the gear lever remote control housing. Its extra bulk prevented the fitting of overdrive in the Magnette without alterations to the transmission tunnel.

A 1960 advert for some of Vic Derrington's tempting products.

The first production car to use the Laycock de Normanville overdrive was the Standard Vanguard of 1948; Jaguar, Austin-Healey and Triumph were among many manufacturers to fit it subsequently, usually as an optional factory extra. MG never offered overdrive on the Magnette, probably because its installation within the transmission tunnel was not straightforward. It was, however, available for after-market fitting and *The Autocar* published a test of a ZB Magnette equipped with a Laycock de Normanville D-type unit that had been installed by the Alexander Engineering Co. in its 22 November 1957 edition.

The overdrive lowered the car's gearing very significantly, from 4.55:1 to 3.44:1 in top gear; it also operated in third gear. The original *Autocar* test had criticised the Magnette's low gearing and the magazine's conclusion was that overdrive 'transforms an already fine small car'. They found that 80–85 mph cruising speeds could be maintained without overworking the engine and a remarkable 31 per cent improvement in fuel consumption was achieved. However, the conversion was not cheap: the overdrive unit cost £94 with a further £15 for fitting.

Victor Derrington was a well-known motorcycle and car racer who was a pioneer in the tuning business, setting up in Kingston, south-west London, in 1923. By the 1950s Derrington was producing a huge variety of after-sales accessories, but of particular interest to Magnette owners would have been the HRG Derrington cross-flow cylinder head

An HRG Derrington cross-flow alloy cylinder head for a B-series engine which was claimed to provide a 20 per cent increase in power. (Photo courtesy of Dominic Taylor-Lane)

The HRG Derrington cylinder head installed in a ZB Magnette along with many other performance goodies, including 1¾-inch SU carburettors, a Derrington-style extractor exhaust manifold and a brake servo. The engine block is an 1800cc 5-bearing B-series and power output is around 115 bhp. (Photo courtesy of Dominic Taylor-Lane)

which, for a cost of £68 10s 0d (assembled, with valves), claimed to provide 20 per cent more power and a 10 per cent saving in fuel consumption. For a further £13 the Magnette owner could buy a Derrington extractor exhaust manifold which, if fitted to the standard engine, was claimed to reduce the ZA's 0–60 mph acceleration time by a full three seconds.

Heady stuff, but did it work? In May 1962 *Practical Motorist* magazine tested a ZA Magnette equipped with the HRG Derrington head and extractor manifold plus a pair of Weber twin-choke 40 DCOE carburettors, high-compression pistons and an MGA camshaft. The car also had the Laycock de Normanville overdrive and a 4.55:1 ZB differential, uprated shock absorbers and a Derrington anti-roll bar, though outwardly it appeared completely standard. The total cost of the extras was a steep £240 (equivalent to over £5,000 in 2018), but the magazine reported a substantial increase in performance – hardly surprising given the engine's output was around 107 bhp compared with the production model's 60 bhp. The 0–60 mph dash was accomplished in 13.8 seconds while the top speed went up from 82 mph to an extremely impressive 107 mph. At 95 mph in overdrive top gear, the engine was spinning at a relatively relaxed 4,000 rpm. Petrol consumption overall was 26 mpg, not dissimilar to the standard model. The report concluded: 'There is, quite definitely, more than a little magnetism about this Magnette.'

8

Racing and Rallying

Motor sport attracted huge interest from the media in the post-war era and British successes were covered by daily newspapers, radio and TV, so involvement offered the chance of free, high-profile publicity for participating manufacturers. A car bathed in the golden glow of success in rallies or on the track would put a spring in the step of the new owner and encourage others into the showroom, justifying the time, money and effort of competing. But then as now it is a high-risk game – setting up and running a works competition team is heavy on resources, and if things go wrong, seeing a new model trounced by competitors is worse than not having competed at all.

MG's last works team had been shut down by Lord Nuffield in 1935, but in late 1954 Leonard Lord, BMC's chairman, was persuaded to merge the Austin and Nuffield competition committees into a new BMC Competitions Department to be based at the MG works in Abingdon. The department's remit was to establish works teams using whichever BMC cars it thought fit. Marcus Chambers, who had managed HRG's racing team before the war, was appointed manager and, with their sporting pedigree, MG's models would have been in the forefront of Chambers' mind.

The Works Rally Team cars and drivers at Monte Carlo, January 1955 (left to right): Reg Holt, Willy Cave, Alan Collinson, Len Shaw, Freddie Finnemore, Geoff Holt, Harold Brooks, and Stan Astbury.

First Outing – The 1955 Monte Carlo Rally

Assembling a team then preparing, testing and de-bugging competition cars takes time. Perhaps anticipating Lord's decision, and before Chambers' appointment, John Thornley had already provisionally entered a team of Magnettes for the January 1955 Monte Carlo Rally. Three maroon ZAs were prepared, these being chassis numbers 3336, 3337 and 3338, bearing registration numbers KJB 908, KJB 909 and KJB 910. The cars were named *Athos, Porthos* and *Aramis,* after the Three Musketeers in Alexandre Dumas's famous book, just like the three victorious works trials cars of 1935 – also Magnettes, but of a rather different style.

The drivers were Reg Holt, Geoff Holt and Len Shaw, accompanied by co-drivers Freddie Finnemore, Alan Collinson and Stan Astbury, who had run a team of three MG YBs in a series of rallies during 1953. For the 1955 works entry two additional co-drivers, Willy Cave and Harold Brooks, were also engaged. Marcus Chambers was thus presented with a *fait accompli* for the first competitive event under his management.

It was not a successful outing. The three cars started from Glasgow on 17 January and faced appalling conditions from the outset with heavy snow, black ice and blocked roads. Two of the three Magnettes carried a three-man crew, and the cars were heavily laden with spares and equipment. To support the extra weight, the rear springs were bound with tape to stiffen them, but on the journey from Glasgow this was found to play havoc with the handling. On arrival in Dover the binding was hastily removed and around 3 cwt of de-ditching equipment was ditched! The handling was much improved but drivers still complained that the 60 bhp at their disposal was not enough, especially for a competitive performance on mountain roads.

The cars struggled through heavy snow in the Alps and made it to Monte Carlo but all three were well down the order – Geoff Holt 178th, Len Shaw 202nd and Reg Holt 237th. Crews were disenchanted with the performance of their cars, and with the support provided by the new Competitions Department, but as this had only been in existence a couple of months it is perhaps not surprising that it still had lessons to learn.

The Grant/Davis works Magnette at the Paris control on the 1956 Monte Carlo Rally. After crashing out on the 1955 rally, Gregor Grant's luck was no better in 1956 when an electrical fault forced the car's retirement. (Photo courtesy of National Motor Museum, Beaulieu)

Several privately entered Magnettes also took part in the 1955 Monte. Six started from Glasgow and five finished, though even further down the order than the works team. The non-finisher was Gregor Grant, the editor of *Autosport*, whose unfortunate encounter with a tree in icy conditions near Grenoble was referred to in Chapter 5.

More Rallying

Athos, Porthos and *Aramis* and their crews were entered in the RAC Rally in March and again struggled in snow, especially on the Welsh sections. Geoff Holt's car won Class 3 (production touring cars 1301–2000cc) and a private entry driven by Whiteaway and Birkett managed third place – some consolation for the disappointment of the Monte.

The final outing for the Three Musketeers team was the 1955 Tulip Rally, run in May. Reg Holt was replaced at the wheel of KJB 908 by Pat Moss, sister of Stirling, who was becoming well known in her own right as a rally driver, while Len Shaw and Geoff Holt piloted the other two cars. Once again success eluded them. Pat Moss's car suffered an oil leak following a pre-rally accident, which caused the engine to seize, while Len Shaw's car suffered a similar fate after overheating, brought about by the combination of a defective radiator blind and a broken temperature gauge. Though Shaw's car struggled on, neither he nor Geoff Holt finished in the awards.

After the frustrations of the 1955 rallies the Three Musketeers team was disbanded but the Competitions Department continued to support Magnette rally entries over the next two years. Gregor Grant once again attempted the Monte in 1956, driving the new works car, JRX 251, which had originally been prepared for circuit racing. The car suffered an electrical failure in France and Grant was forced to retire. On the same event, Nancy Mitchell, partnered by Doreen Reece and Susan Hindmarsh, drove KJB 910 from the Stockholm start point and managed 59th overall and third place in the ladies' cup.

Nancy Mitchell (left) receives an award from John Thornley, MG's general manager. Marcus Chambers (centre) and John Gott (right) look on. (Photo courtesy of MGCC)

Nancy Mitchell's 1956 Monte drive presaged some notable successes for women drivers. Mitchell herself, driving a variety of works Magnettes and MGAs, won the European Ladies' Rally Championship for 1956, while Pat Moss and Ann Wisdom drove MBL 417, a newly prepared ZA, to second place in the ladies' cup on the Dieppe Rally.

For 1957 the Competitions Department prepared a new ZB: NJB 365. In this car Nancy Mitchell achieved a second in the ladies' cup on the Sestrières Rally and a third in the Tulip Rally. She won the ladies' cup on the Alpine Rally driving an MGA and at the end of the season was awarded the European Ladies' Rally Championship cup for a second year.

The Monte Carlo Rally was reinstated in 1958 after being cancelled in 1957 as a result of the Suez Crisis and works Magnettes reappeared in familiar hands. However, both Nancy Mitchell's and Gregor Grant's cars were involved in accidents and, while Grant struggled to the finish, he was out of time. David Seigle-Morris and Johnny Reeves, driving a new Varitone with works support, also finished too late and in April they retired from the Tulip Rally.

By 1958 the Competitions Department had a new and highly effective rallying weapon in their armoury, the Austin-Healey 100-6, so the Magnette was superseded. As a rally car it had appeared to show much promise and, though some drivers complained of a lack of power, rallies of the time were seldom decided on differences of fractions of a second. Consistency and reliability are the keys to success in long-distance events, from driver, machine and team, and such characteristics are not generated overnight. The BMC Competitions Department took a few years to become fully effective and, in retrospect, the early years were a learning period which set the foundations for the glory days of the big Healeys and little Minis from the late 1950s.

Racing Successes

Somewhat surprisingly the Magnette proved to be a more successful circuit racer than rally car, largely thanks to the efforts of driver and team manager Dick Jacobs.

Jacobs came from a motoring pedigree. Born in 1916, his father had established Mill Garage in South Woodford on the Essex/London border in 1919 and as a lad before the Second World War he was the proud owner of an MG J2 and later a TA Midget. In 1946 Mill Garage was appointed an MG dealer and, armed with a new TC Midget, Jacobs began competing in club motor sport.

After success in a variety of MGs over several seasons, his friendship with John Thornley led to involvement in the 'semi-official' MG works team from 1952. Driving a YB saloon, Jacobs won his class in the 1952, 1953 and 1954 Daily Express Touring Car Race held annually at Silverstone.

Jacobs had hoped to run a ZA Magnette in the 1954 race but the works was still suffering from production problems, so he had to persist with the YB. But the next year, with the Competitions Department now established, he was invited to drive JRX 251, the works ZA. Early testing at Silverstone proved promising, and to show he meant business Jacobs set himself a punishing training regime. He explained: 'I cut down on cigarettes, stopped drinking and six days a week I went to a boating lake and hired the heaviest rowing boat they had for an hour!'[1]

1. Dick Jacobs, *An MG Experience,* 1976 (See Bibliography)

Perhaps not quite the regime of modern track stars, but it worked. In the 1955 *Daily Express* Touring Car Race, held on 7 May, Jacobs' Magnette won its class at an average speed of 71.45 mph (nearly 5 mph faster than his YB the year before) and two privately entered Magnettes, driven by Alan Foster and John Waller, were second and third.

The Competitions Department had entered three MGA prototypes for the 1955 Le Mans 24-hour race and, in light of his success, Jacobs was invited to be one of the drivers. But less than three hours into the race his good fortune deserted him and, in the immediate aftermath of the notorious accident in which one of the Mercedes team cars ploughed into the crowd, killing more than eighty spectators, he lost control of his MGA and crashed, sustaining severe injuries.

After four months in hospital, Jacobs resolved that he would not race again, instead turning his hand to team management. Alan Foster was engaged to drive the works ZA Magnette in the 1956 *Daily Express* saloon car race, once again held in May at Silverstone. The event produced a tight battle for the 1500cc class between Foster and Reg Parnell. Driving a Borgward Isabella, Parnell won by just one second.

In August, Jacobs entered a non-works team of five Magnettes for the 750 Motor Club's six-hour relay race. Drivers were Alan Foster, Harold Rumsey, John Waller, Mike Edmondson and Peter Clarke and they finished victorious, beating the Triumph TR2 and the 750 Motor Club teams into second and third places.

The following year the *Daily Express* saloon car race was held in September and Jacobs entered a team of three Magnettes driven by Alan Foster, John Waller and Roy Bloxham. Things went better than in 1956, with Foster and Waller taking first and second places in their class.

The BRSCC British Saloon Car Championship, precursor to today's British Touring Car Championship, was first run in 1958 with nine rounds of racing around the country. Jacobs prepared a modified ZB Magnette for Alan Foster, entered in Class B (1201–1600cc), while John Waller ran his own car (registered 21 JPU) prepared to a similar specification. In the first two rounds, at Brands Hatch and Aintree, Foster won his class but he crashed heavily at Silverstone in May after losing a wheel, wrecking the car. John Waller nobly

John Waller cornering hard during the 1955 Daily Express Touring Car Race held at Silverstone. Waller finished 3rd in class behind the Magnettes of Dick Jacobs and Alan Foster. (Photo courtesy of National Motor Museum, Beaulieu)

sold 21 JPU to Foster so he could complete the season, Waller's reasoning being that, as a dental surgeon, he could not afford to lose his livelihood should he injure a hand in an accident! In this car, Foster went on to win Class B for 1958, finishing fifth overall in the championship behind the winning Austin A105 driven by Jack Sears, Tommy Sopwith's 3.4-litre Jaguar and a brace of Austin A35s.

As in rallying, 1958 was the final year in which works Magnettes competed on the track. The Competitions Department turned to Austin A35s, A40s and the new Riley 1.5, and then, as the 1960s dawned, to the all-conquering Minis. Dick Jacobs, meanwhile, concentrated his skills on a team running the new MGA Twin-Cam sports cars.

Alan Foster driving the ex-John Waller ZB at Silverstone in July 1958 on his way to a class win in the BRSCC British Saloon Car Championship.

Magnettes were, and remain, popular in more light-hearted club events too! (Gordon Horner sketch provided by Warren Marsh)

Postscript – Racing to a Glorious Death

By the late 1960s a Magnette was just another old car, rapidly succumbing to mechanical maladies and terminal corrosion. Cars could be bought for buttons and run into the ground before being despatched to a scrapyard.

For a brief few years in the 1960s and 1970s, Magnettes saw a revival of their glory days on the track. This time it was not on the famous circuits of Silverstone, Aintree, Goodwood or Brands Hatch, but in places whose names had a less familiar ring – Wimbledon, Matchams Park, Northampton, the 440-yard oval tracks built in the 1950s for the new sports of stock car and banger racing. While stock cars were purpose-built racing machines, the bangers were just as the name implied – old cars that had been sent to the scrapyard but which still had enough life in them for a final few glory laps around the track. This was a no-holds-barred contact sport, and the crowds revelled in the huge pile-ups which ensued. The grand finale was the 'Destruction Derby' in which the last car moving was declared the winner.

Even in old age the Magnette's relative speed and strength meant that it was a popular choice among the drivers, and for a while no race was complete without at least one Magnette battling for the winner's laurels. However, by the late 1970s the supply of scrap Magnettes was drying up and for a while the Magnette's competition role was over.

Jan Pearce was one of the pioneers who revived the Magnette as a popular car for classic events. Here, his ZB is seen on the 1995 Monte Carlo Challenge. John Heffer is the co-driver. (Photo courtesy of David Halliday)

9

Renaissance

Decline and Fall

Old cars die for a couple of reasons. The first is a matter of simple economics. As they get older, their value falls and eventually a mechanical malaise, an accident or the cost of passing the annual safely check will exceed the value of the car.

The second is the drying up of the supply of spare parts. As numbers decline, the original manufacturer will no longer find it worthwhile to supply spares, so even a relatively minor mishap may result in the car becoming unusable.

In the UK in the early 1970s a sound, well-maintained Magnette was worth perhaps £250 while a runner, which might keep the purchaser mobile for a year or two, could be had for £50. A Magnette thus offered cheap motoring with a certain style – the badge proudly mounted on the grille spoke of a long and glorious pedigree and the coachwork's elegant

End of the road? A derelict Magnette awaits its fate in the company of a 1930s Austin 7 Ruby. (Photo courtesy of David Halliday)

The lowest point in the Magnette's fortunes? A ZB is smashed up by a street gang in The Who's 1973 album *Quadrophenia*.

lines stood out from the humdrum styles of the day. But with such low values an owner had to have a very good reason – or relentless enthusiasm – to resist the call of the scrapyard when a problem arose.

The situation was not helped by the UK Ministry of Transport's annual MOT test, which had been introduced in 1960 and was becoming ever more draconian. From 1977 testers were required to check a vehicle's structure and, given the propensity of the Magnette bodyshell to rust, thousands more cars were condemned.

A strange footnote to the Magnette's decline was provided by The Who's rock opera *Quadrophenia,* which was about a young, disillusioned mod, Jimmy, seeking a reason for existence in Brighton and London. The double album, released in October 1973, included a thirty-two-page pull-out of grainy black and white photos of the plot, three of which show Jimmy and his gang smashing up a sad-looking ZB Magnette in a grimy London street. In the final shot the car lies overturned, windows smashed, as the lads make their escape.

Resurrection

The first seeds of hope for Magnette admirers had already been planted nine years before *Quadrophenia*. In 1964, dedicated owner Lou Shorten set up a small business in Norfolk to provide Magnette owners with parts and restoration services. A determined and motivated lady, Lou had bought her ZA Magnette in 1957. At the time, she was working on a farm and the car had a hard life, carrying anything from half a ton of poultry feed to, on one memorable occasion, a six-month-old Hereford calf which travelled hobbled on the back seat for more than 40 miles.

In 1964, and by now working in a garage, Lou taught herself to rebuild the Magnette's engine, to use a paint sprayer and to repair bodywork. With the supply of spare parts drying up, she also started collecting cars that were beyond repair. Thus began 'MG Specialists

Lou Shorten, who set up her unique business repairing, maintaining and supplying parts for Magnettes in 1964, pictured in front of the workshop in Norfolk in which she and her husband John brought countless Magnettes back to life. (Photo courtesy of Magnette Register Archives)

John and Lou Shorten at Silverstone in 1980. Lou was also the proud owner of the F-type Magna pictured. (Photo courtesy of Magnette Register Archives)

The very first meeting of Magnette enthusiasts was held at Donnington Park circuit in 1971. (Photo courtesy of Magnette Register Archives)

Lenwade', which became the leading parts supplier and restorer for Magnette enthusiasts across the globe. Lou, aided by her husband John, ran the business until her death in 2015, becoming the world's leading authority on the model in the process. Peter Martin took over the business and continues the invaluable service to Magnette owners that Lou started more than half a century ago.

In 1974, the MG Car Club, acknowledging the growing acceptance of the Magnette by enthusiasts, set up a Magnette Register whose aims were to help and support owners, to develop and disseminate specialist knowledge and advice, to keep a record of surviving cars and to organise events for owners. With a source of parts to keep the cars going and club support for the enthusiastic owner, the Magnette's long decline was finally being reversed.

With momentum building, the Magnette began to attract the attention of the specialist press. Britain's original classic car magazine, *Thoroughbred and Classic Cars,* established in 1973, published a history and buyer's guide for the Magnette in September 1977. Its main rival, *Classic and Sports Car,* was first published in April 1982 and ran a guide to the Magnette in its January 1983 edition.

Recognition

By the mid-1980s the Magnette had become a firm favourite among the burgeoning classic car fraternity. The reasons for its popularity were essentially the same as those that had made it attractive in the 1950s – its coachwork spoke of a departed age of grace and elegance while its performance, though modest by 1980s standards, was still perfectly adequate to keep pace with the traffic of the day. Driveability and handling were on a par with cars thirty years younger and if the owner wished for a bit more power, there was ample scope for tuning. Well-maintained examples were both reliable and practical enough to be used as everyday family transport.

Press articles of the time often referred to the Magnette as 'the forgotten MG', and it was certainly the sports cars that tended to attract most attention. This may be one of the reasons why, despite its many merits, the Magnette was something of a bargain in the classic car world. Even by the mid-1980s, when the classic car movement was in full swing, excellent examples could be had for less than £2,000. This was less than half the value of an MGA, which had been the cheaper car when new. Low values were, though, something of a double-edged sword; on the plus side, it meant the Magnette was an accessible classic which many could afford to buy and not be afraid to use. On the downside, restoration costs could often far exceed the value of a good car, so numbers continued to diminish as cars were still scrapped or broken up for parts.

Fast-forward three decades and the classic car movement continues to go from strength to strength. It has also changed fundamentally. No longer is the average purchaser someone armed with boundless enthusiasm but limited cash, aiming to find stylish transport for the price of an 'old banger'. Classic cars are part of the burgeoning nostalgia industry, an accessory in which to be seen at Lord March's Goodwood Revival in Sussex or on the manicured lawns of California's Pebble Beach. With the prices of the most valuable models in the tens of millions (a 1962 Ferrari 250 GTO achieved $48.4 million at Sotheby's auction in Monterey, California, in 2018), some are now works of art to be treasured as investments rather than used as a means of transport.

MGs, mass-produced in their tens of thousands, do not inhabit the same world as such exotica, but their values have escalated in line with the booming market. The very best Magnettes, those capable of winning a *concours d'elegance* prize, can achieve in excess of £20,000 in the UK while useable examples that would benefit from some improvement can fetch upwards of £5,000. A Magnette is no longer a cheap run-around, but it has proved to be an excellent investment. In the twenty-first century, when the stock markets have peaked, crashed and staggered back to around where they started, Magnette values have doubled, more than justifying a modest investment in classic engineering – and who has had fun driving a pile of share certificates?

Today, then, the ownership profile has changed from the impecunious young enthusiast to the older owner with a little spare cash to spend on a hobby. In consequence, the typical Magnette will take to the road on a fine summer's day but very few are in regular daily use. With rising values, though, more are being restored and the number of roadworthy cars is increasing, supported by a burgeoning classic car industry which now generates revenues in excess of £5.5 billion in the UK alone.[1] With a range of skilled restorers, mechanics and parts suppliers now available, Magnette ownership has never been better supported.

'What price when <u>they</u> want to buy?' Gordon Horner's prediction, in a sketch made at an early Magnette rally in 1977, showed amazing foresight! (Sketch provided by Warren Marsh)

1. Federation of British Historic Vehicle Clubs' National Historic Vehicle Survey 2016.

This immaculate Twilight Grey 1955 ZA is owned by Grant Howlett. It was bought new by his grandfather and is entirely original, having never been altered or restored. (Photo courtesy of Grant Howlett)

Five seats and a big boot – the perfect classic for all the family! (Photo courtesy of David Halliday)

10

Magnettes in the Twenty-first Century

Buying a Magnette

Of the 36,600 Magnettes produced, the MG Car Club Magnette Register has details of some 2,000 cars, many of which are still in existence, though by no means are all roadworthy. This is a surprisingly high survival rate and there will usually be a choice of cars available to buy, from concours examples to those requiring complete restoration. Finding a good car can, however, be challenging.

It makes sense to buy the best you can afford. The one certainty of classic car restoration is that it will be more complex, time consuming and costly than expected. Despite rising values, restoration can still cost more than the completed car is worth, so it pays to find a car in as good a condition, and requiring as little work, as possible.

The condition of the bodywork is key. Gerald Palmer designed the car around a strong monocoque shell, the rigidity and stiffness of which contributed to the excellent handling characteristics. It is, however, very susceptible to rust, especially along the seams and within the inaccessible box sections. Cars of the 1950s were built with scant regard for, and a lack of understanding of, rust prevention; protection was limited to conventional paint finishes applied to whatever was visible. As a result, when water penetrates box sections, doors and areas of double-skinning it becomes trapped and corrosion begins from within. By the time blisters appear externally, damage to the structure can be well advanced.

The first areas to check are the sills and box sections running between the front and rear wheels. These are structural and, in bad cases, rust here can cause the whole body to distort. The front hangers for the rear springs are attached to the rear of the box section on either side and these too can corrode badly. Repairs here are difficult and expensive, but easy to bodge.

The floor of the passenger compartment can also disintegrate, especially along its outer edges. This is easier to repair but the job must be done well – check that the floor has the correct stiffening pressings in it and is not simply a sheet of flat metal.

The rear wheel arches are double-skinned and rust around the arch itself and in the lower part of the wing behind the rear wheel. The section of the wheel arch exposed when the rear door is opened is partly double-skinned and should also be checked carefully.

This picture shows the right-hand side of a badly rusted car. The sill, floor and most of the structural box section have all suffered serious corrosion and been cut away. Temporary bracing bars have been welded across the door openings to prevent the whole structure distorting under its own weight. Work on replacing the metalwork has begun on the right of the picture. (Photo courtesy of Peter Martin)

The front hanger for the rear spring on the same car. This area is structurally vital and will need a lot of skilled work to restore it to full strength. (Photo courtesy of Peter Martin)

The boot floor can rust if boot seals have failed and the boot lid will corrode along its lower edge, but second-hand lids can still be found.

The front wings will rust around the headlights, along the bottom edges and along a seam running from the top of the headlight rearwards to the inner edge of the wing. The bonnet rarely suffers serious corrosion but the doors can rot badly along the bottom edges, especially when drain holes become blocked.

Repair sections are available for practically all rust-prone panels, but fitting them requires a high level of skill. It is relatively easy to hide areas of corrosion and poor workmanship behind layers of body filler and shiny paint, so even the smartest-looking bodywork should be scrupulously checked.

The interior of a Magnette is also costly to restore. If the leatherwork requires replacement, expect an upholsterer's bill of at least £2,000. Wood finishes can be damaged by water leaks or prolonged exposure to the sun, causing the veneer to lift and crack. Repairs can again be expensive, though this is a job that the skilled home restorer can tackle, and the results can be very satisfying. Replacement headlining is available, as are good-quality carpets.

Mechanically, there is less to worry about. The B-series engine has a reputation for toughness and longevity, spare parts are generally readily available and there are many experts with the knowledge and skill to undertake a repair or rebuild. Check for excessive

The bottom of the rear wing showing typical corrosion. (Photo courtesy of Peter Martin)

blue or white smoke from the exhaust, pointing towards cylinder bore wear or a leaking head gasket, and listen carefully for rumbling or knocking from the engine, indicating big-end or crankshaft bearing problems. Breakdowns are generally caused by relatively minor electrical or fuel supply issues, a root cause of which is often the poor quality of cheap modern reproduction components.

Expect some moderate gearbox whine in first, second and third gears – that's just how they are! The change itself should be quick and positive. Regular faults are confined to weak synchromesh on second gear and a tendency for third gear to pop out into neutral on the overrun. There is no synchromesh on first gear. Parts are available should a rebuild be required.

The differential can become noisy but rarely suffers serious problems. On high-mileage cars, worn seals can cause leakage from the axle onto the rear brake linings, reducing braking efficiency. New seals are available, though sometimes the hubs will also require repair.

On the road, the car should handle tautly and there should be no lost motion in the steering. Worn suspension bushes can cause the handling and ride to deteriorate; replacements are available in rubber or polyurethane. The front suspension tie rods can be prone to failure where they attach to the frame of the car and should be carefully checked. The telescopic dampers can leak and lose their efficiency, but modern alternatives are available.

Modifying the Magnette – Gilding the Lily?

There are two distinct schools of thought when it comes to modifying a classic car. Some believe a car should remain unmodified, a faithful testament to its creators and its period. The mechanical components, colour, upholstery and other finishes should match the original specification and any accessories should be limited to those available at the time the car was produced. The rules of most *concours d'elegance* competitions will provide for marks to be deducted if the car has been modified. On the other hand, many consider that improvements to a car's performance, braking and handling are thoroughly worthwhile, enabling it to be used more effectively and safely in modern traffic conditions.

This purposeful-looking car with lowered suspension, wider wheels and many other modifications was originally an all-black Varitone. The engine, an 1800cc MGB unit with an HRG Derrington cross-flow cylinder head plus other modifications, is pictured in Chapter 7. (Photo courtesy of Dominic Taylor-Lane)

Modifying a Magnette in the twenty-first century is the continuation of a long tradition stretching back more than six decades. Books have been published on B-series engine tuning and the MGCC Magnette Register website[1] includes a section on how to undertake many popular modifications. Reference should be made to these and other relevant sources for detailed guidance on how to undertake such work; the remainder of this chapter illustrates some of the options available.

Upping the Power of the B-Series

Starting with the standard 1,489cc engine, the ZA's modest 60 bhp was increased to 68 bhp in the ZB by fitting larger carburettors, a better exhaust manifold and higher compression pistons. A ZA can be uprated to ZB specification, giving a useful 13 per cent increase in power.

For more comprehensive modification to the original engine one can simply follow the path taken by the engine tuners of the 1950s. As outlined in Chapter 7, well over 100 bhp can be coaxed out of a 1,489cc B-series engine in this way. The HRG Derrington aluminium cross-flow cylinder head is being reproduced in the twenty-first century, as is a copy of the tubular steel Derrington exhaust manifold, so this is a viable option, though expensive – the price of components alone could substantially exceed £2,000.

A simpler and cheaper alternative is to replace the 1,489cc engine with one of the later and more powerful versions of the B-series. The choices are the 1,588cc unit fitted to the MGA 1600, the 1,622cc engine found in the MGA 1600 Mk II and later Farina saloons, the 1,798cc three-bearing MGB engine and the 1,798cc five-bearing engine fitted to later MGBs and Morris Marinas. Standard power outputs varied according to the car in which the engine was installed and ranged from around 60 bhp in basic form to 95 bhp in the MGB. For the MGB engine, modifications to the cylinder head, pistons, carburettors, exhaust manifold etc. can increase power to around 110 bhp without loss of reliability and more than 150 bhp can be coaxed from the five-bearing engine in full race tune.

1. MGCC Magnette Register website: www.magnette.org.

Because the dimensions of all the three-bearing engines are basically the same, installation in a Magnette is straightforward. Although fitting a five-bearing engine is a little more complicated, the benefit is a stronger and probably longer-lasting unit that is capable of taking a higher level of tune.

Some More Radical Options

If 110 bhp is considered a bit tame for a 1950s saloon car, then why not follow in the footsteps of several enterprising owners and ditch the old-fashioned B-series engine in favour of a more up-to-date power plant?

To take one rather exciting example, Darren Brock's 1954 Magnette ZA has been in his family since 1957 and, keen to combine his enthusiasm for the Mercedes-Benz marque with his ownership of the Magnette, he installed a 1997cc Mercedes-Benz engine and gearbox built for the DTM (German Touring Car) championship. With more than 300 bhp available, the remainder of the car had to be upgraded to match; modifications include reworked rear suspension, wider wheels from a Triumph TR6 and disc brakes all round. What is truly remarkable, however, is what has not been needed – Palmer's front suspension design remains essentially unchanged and the bodywork is basically 'stock', barring some subtle bracing. The interior still sports the timber dash and original instruments, augmented by a substantial tachometer. A true testament to the 'rightness' of the original design!

Back in the 1970s British Leyland produced around 2,600 MGB GTs with the all-aluminium Rover/Buick 3500cc V8 engine, transforming a perfectly pleasant small sports car into a true grand tourer. So why not do the same in the Magnette? Several enterprising owners have proved that this is possible with a little ingenuity. Andrew de Bernes' car is a particularly fine example, whose 3,900cc V8 engine produces a very smooth 200 hp and drives the rear wheels via a five-speed Rover gearbox. The bodywork and interior have been very tastefully customised and the result is a unique machine with outstanding performance and striking appearance.

Darren Brock's 300+ bhp Magnette-Mercedes in the paddock at Crystal Palace. (Photo courtesy of Malcom Eades)

Above left: The Mercedes-Benz DTM engine is a tight fit in the Magnette's engine compartment! (Photo courtesy of Malcom Eades)

Above right: Apart from the seats, the interior of Darren Brock's car is surprisingly original. (Photo courtesy of Malcom Eades)

Above left: Andrew de Bernes' fabulous V8-powered 1955 ZA Magnette. (Photo courtesy of Andrew de Bernes)

Above right: The 3,900cc Rover/TVR engine snugly installed beneath the Magnette's bonnet. (Photo courtesy of Andrew de Bernes)

Far from original but a delight to the eye – the interior of Andrew de Bernes' V8 Magnette. (Photo courtesy of Andrew de Bernes)

Transmission

The principal criticism of the Magnette's transmission has always been its low gearing. To overcome this, the simplest and cheapest solution is to install a higher ratio differential and, as with engines, there are several alternatives. A 4.3:1 axle ratio was fitted to most MGAs and BMC Farina saloons, the MGA 1600 Mk II was 4.1:1 and MGBs were 3.9:1. These can all be fitted into the Magnette's rear axle, though most will need to have their drive gears swapped to fit the coarser splines of the Magnette half shafts.

A better approach, albeit more expensive and complicated, is to install an MGB overdrive gearbox. This requires alteration of the transmission tunnel, gearbox support bracket and exhaust, a new propshaft and a revised speedometer drive, but once this is completed high-speed cruising will be quieter, more economical and much more relaxing.

A more modern alternative is to fit a five-speed gearbox. The most popular option is the Ford Type 9, which was used in Capris, Sierras and Merkurs from the mid-1980s. Built in the hundreds of thousands, it is a strong unit with well-spaced ratios. Hi-Gear Engineering Ltd in the UK provide a complete installation kit for the Magnette[2] which requires minimal alteration to the bodywork.

In Australia and the USA, a number of cars have been adapted to take the five-speed gearbox from the Datsun/Nissan 280Z which may be mated to the MGB five-bearing engine using a purpose-built back plate.

Brakes

The Magnette's standard drum brakes were very effective by the standards of its day and, if in good condition and correctly set up, they are perfectly adequate for modern road conditions. The brake pedal requires more effort than in a modern car, but to reduce this

Front suspension showing a disc brake conversion and an original Derrington anti-roll bar which is bolted to the lower suspension arm and mounted to the chassis rail via a purpose-made bracket. (Author)

2. Hi-Gear Engineering: www.hi-gearengineering.co.uk.

a servo can be fitted. It will not, by itself, improve the car's stopping ability but Magnette brakes can be upgraded by replacing the front drums with more modern disc brakes, which are less prone to brake fade and do not need adjusting. The conversion employs MGB callipers and back plates, as well as MGA discs and hubs, plus a purpose-made mounting plate. Patterns are available and small batches are occasionally manufactured by specialist machine shops.

Suspension

The Magnette's suspension needs little upgrading even for use on twenty-first-century roads and it can readily cope with a significant increase in performance. There are, however, some useful tweaks that can be carried out.

Derrington manufactured a front anti-roll (sway) bar as an after-market accessory in the 1950s which reduced body roll during cornering, further improving the handling. The bar and its fittings have not been manufactured for many decades and originals are extremely rare, but a reproduction based on the original patterns has been produced in recent years.

Polyurethane suspension bushes are available which distort less under load by comparison with the original rubber bushes and thus improve steering response and handling. Polyurethane has a longer service life, though its benefits can be at the expense of a slightly harsher ride and increased transmission of road noise. The original Girling telescopic dampers have proved extremely long-lasting in service but can be replaced by modern alternatives if necessary.

Wheels and Tyres

The vast majority of Magnettes retain their perforated steel wheels which suit the car well, finished as they are with chrome hubcaps sporting a central MG logo. Very occasionally they can develop cracks which can lead to failure in extreme circumstances.

BMC became aware of the potential weaknesses of these wheels, which were also fitted to early MGAs, in 1958. The MGA 1600 was equipped with a slightly different design of wheel which incorporated oval rather than round ventilation holes and these may be fitted to a Magnette – only the most eagle-eyed enthusiast would spot the difference. For racing and rallying, the perforated steel disc wheels fitted to early Saab 99s provide a stronger alternative that looks similar to the original wheel, though the hubcaps cannot be fitted. Triumph TR6 steel wheels will also fit, again without hubcaps. Both the Saab and Triumph alternatives are wider than the original Magnette wheels, allowing for the fitting of wider tyres.

Contemporary MGAs had the option of wire wheels and some Magnettes have been converted using MGA 1500 front hubs (unless disc brakes are fitted) and an MGA rear axle. There is no doubt that a Magnette fitted with wire wheels looks great, though wires are not as strong and require more maintenance (and much more cleaning!) than standard steel wheels.

Though not an option when new, wire wheels undoubtedly look good on a Magnette. (Photo courtesy of Robin Lawton)

Magnettes were originally equipped with 5.60 x 15 cross-ply tyres. These are still available from specialist suppliers but modern radial tyres offer better grip, a longer life and are cheaper. The usual size for a Magnette is 165/80 R15.

Electrical

The majority of breakdowns are brought about by electrical failure – not for nothing was the electrical components manufacturer Lucas known as 'the Prince of Darkness'! Consequently, most of the electrical upgrades to the Magnette are aimed at building reliability into a system which had its origins in the 1930s.

The original dynamo, regulated by an electro-mechanical control box, may be replaced by an alternator, which is generally more reliable and does not need a separate control box. A further benefit is improved output when operating at low speeds. If original under-bonnet appearance is important, a Dynalite alternator, purpose-built within the body of a dynamo, can be fitted.

The ignition system is probably the greatest source of trouble on any car from the 1950s, with the distributor being the likeliest culprit. Fortunately, a number of manufacturers make electronic ignition systems that can be built into the standard Lucas 25D distributor, eliminating the points and condenser, which are the usual causes of failure. Programmable ignition systems can also offer much finer control of the ignition timing than is provided by the springs and centrifugal weights in the original distributor.

Moving from reliability to safety in modern traffic, the most common modification is the installation of flashing indicators to replace the semaphore trafficators. Owners have devised an enormous variety of ways to do this, the trick being to find an installation that is both effective and pleasing to look at – adding additional lights to the Magnette's smooth profile can be an aesthetic challenge.

The original Lucas P700 7-inch headlights with their distinctive tripod support for the reflector look great but they produce a rather narrow beam which, on a dark and rainy night, can make driving a little too exciting. The standard Lucas H4 7-inch headlight used in dozens of British makes and models from the 1950s to the 1980s provides a much

Above left: One way of installing amber flashing indicators on a Magnette ... (Photo courtesy of Alan Cleobury)

Above right: ... and another. (Author)

better beam, especially when fitted with a halogen bulb conversion kit. Halogen and, more recently, LED bulbs are available for other lights on the car – their use in tail/stop lights is especially recommended.

Seatbelts

Driving a Magnette in modern traffic, surrounded by vehicles equipped with multiple air bags, automatic braking and ABS, crumple zones and a plethora of other safety-related paraphernalia, inevitably turns one's thoughts to the installation of seatbelts. Fortunately, this job is relatively straightforward and inertia reel belts for all four seats can be fitted after suitable mounting points have been installed.

A Summary

In the mid-1950s the Magnette was an advanced car offering above average performance and a high level of equipment. An unmodified car can still be used perfectly well on modern roads and many prefer to preserve their cars as they were manufactured.

If enhanced performance is required, modifications can be readily and relatively cheaply undertaken by using components from later BMC models which developed the engineering that was largely pioneered in the Magnette. The car's basic structure, suspension and steering are more than capable of coping with increases in power output of at least 50 per cent. A modified car will be able to keep pace with twenty-first-century traffic and can undertake long journeys in comfort. For those concerned about a loss of originality, most of the modifications are readily reversible if the original components are kept.

And so, seventy years on from its conception, a Magnette can still provide regular and practical transport in style for its owner and the whole family – a tribute to the 'rightness' of Palmer's original design and to the ingenuity of owners over the decades. Who knows what the next seven decades will bring? One thing is for sure – Magnettes will roll on and, if necessary, someone, somewhere will devise a battery-powered conversion!

And finally, something completely different! When a garage roof collapsed on this Varitone the owner decided to chop it off and create a unique convertible. (Author)

Appendix 1

MG Magnette ZA and ZB specifications, technical data and performance figures:

Engine: BMC B-series, four cylinders in-line, cast-iron engine block and cylinder head. Three-bearing crankshaft with shell-type bearings. Overhead valves operated by push-rods and rockers from chain-driven camshaft located in engine block.

Bore/stroke: 73.025mm/88.9mm. Capacity: 1,489cc. Compression ratio: 15GA engine (most ZAs) 7.15:1; 15GC engine (late ZA and ZB) 8.3:1.

Maximum power: 15GA, 60 bhp at 4,600 rpm; 15GC, 68 bhp at 5,200 rpm.

Maximum torque: 15GA, 76.1–78 lb ft at 3,000 rpm; 15GC, 83lb ft at 3,000 rpm

Fuel system: Twin SU carburettors (Most ZAs: type H2 1¼ inch; late ZAs and ZBs: type H4 1½ inch). SU electric fuel pump. Fuel tank capacity 9.25 gallons.

Cooling system: Pressurised, with engine-driven fan and pump, thermostatically controlled. Capacity 10.5 pints.

Ignition system: Battery, coil and Lucas 25D distributor, automatic advance and retard.

Transmission: Front engine, rear-wheel drive. Clutch: single 8-inch dry plate, hydraulic operation. Gearbox: Four forward speeds and reverse, synchromesh on second, third and fourth gears, remote control gear lever. Rear axle: three-quarter floating axle with hypoid bevel differential. Final drive ratio: 4.875:1 (cars with 15GA engine) or 4.55:1 (cars with 15GC engine).

Suspension: Front: Independent with upper wishbone and lower arm, front and rear reaction arms. Live rear axle mounted on semi-elliptic leaf springs. Girling telescopic shock absorbers.

Steering: Rack and pinion, 2.75 turns lock-to-lock. Turning circle: 37.5 feet.

Brakes: Lockheed hydraulic single circuit system, 10x1.75-inch drums, twin leading shoes to front brakes, leading and trailing shoes to rear. Cable-operated handbrake on rear drums from central lever.

Wheels and tyres: Four-stud ventilated disc wheels, size 4x15 inches with cross ply 5.50x15 tyres.

Electrical: 12 V system with single 51Ah rating battery. Positive earth. Charging system: Lucas DM2 dynamo, automatic voltage regulator.

Instruments: Speedometer with total and trip distance recorders, fuel, oil pressure, water temperature and ammeter gauges, electric clock.

Bodywork: Four-door, four/five seat saloon, all-steel unitary construction. Leather-faced upholstery. Heater and ventilation system standard on UK cars, optional in most export markets.

Dimensions: Wheelbase: 102 inches, track: 51 inches, overall length: 169 inches, overall width: 63 inches, overall height: 58 inches, kerb weight: 2,464 lb.

Performance figures: Maximum speed: Cars with 15GA engine: 80 mph; 15GC engine: 86.5 mph. Acceleration 0–50 mph (standing quarter-mile in brackets): 15GA engine: 15.6 (22.7) seconds; 15GC engine: 13.0 (21.6) seconds. Fuel consumption: 24-32mpg (15GA), 23-30mpg (15GC).

Appendix 2

Production Numbers

	ZA	Standard ZB	Varitone ZB	Total
1953	8			8
1954	3,823			3,823
1955	8,925			8,925
1956	5,320	1,683	382	7,385
1957		4,256	2,740	6,996
1958		4,783	4,655	9,438
1959			26	26
Total	18,076	10,722	7,803	36,601

Appendix 3

Magnette Identification

The Magnette Vehicle Identification Number (VIN, also known as chassis number) comprises three or four letters followed by two numbers and finally a number of between three and five digits e.g. KAB 13 14714. The code identifies the car as follows:

First letter: Always K, identifying the car as an MG Magnette.

Second letter: Describes the body style. 'A' stands for four-door saloon so this was the second letter for all Magnettes.

Third letter: Identifies colour. A=black, B=light grey, C=dark red, D=dark blue, E=mid green, F=beige, G=brown, H=primer finish (for CKD cars), J=dark grey, K=light red, L=light blue, P=ivory, R=white, S=mid grey, T=light green, U=dark green (NB – not all the above colours were offered on Magnettes).

Fourth letter: Identifies second colour on Varitone cars.

First number: 1=RHD home market; 2=RHD export; 3=LHD North America export; 5=RHD CKD ('Completely knocked down' i.e. car exported in parts for assembly outside the UK); 6=LHD CKD.

Second number: Paint type – 1=synthetic; 3=cellulose; 4=metallic; 5=primer (CKD cars).

Final number: Car or production number. The first production car was numbered 501 and the last was 37101.

As an example, KAB 13 14714 can therefore be identified as an MG Magnette with four-door saloon bodywork with single-colour light grey cellulose paint. It was an RHD home-market car and the 14,214th built (because the first production car was No. 501) and its approximate built date would have been February/March 1956, which may be estimated using the table below.

Date	Car No.	Event
September 1953	501	First production car
January 1954	537	First car commenced in 1954
January 1955	4332	First car commenced in 1955
January 1956	13257	First car commenced in 1956
July 1956	18101	First ZA with ZB-specification engine and transmission
September 1956	18576	Last ZA
September 1956	18577	First ZB
October 1956	18605	First ZB Varitone
January 1957	20642	First car in 1957
January 1958	27638	First car in 1958
January 1959	37101	Last car produced

Appendix 4

Magnette colour combinations:

Single Colour Cars

Body Colour	Seats and Trim	Carpet	Dates of Production	VIN Code
Metallic green	Biscuit	Green	Oct 1953 to Oct 1954	U
	Green	Green		
Metallic Twilight Grey	Grey	Red	Oct 1953 to Oct 1954	J
	Maroon	Red		
Autumn Red	Biscuit	Red	Oct 1953 to Oct 1955	C
	Maroon	Red		
Black	Biscuit	Red	Oct 1953 to Dec 1958	A
	Maroon	Red		
	Green	Green		
	Grey	Grey		
MG Green	Biscuit	Green	Oct 1954 to Sept 1955	U
	Green	Green		

Twilight Grey	Grey	Red	Oct 1954 to Dec 1958	J
	Maroon	Red		
Steel Blue	Maroon	Grey	Jul 1955 to Dec 1958	L
	Black	Grey		
Royal Tan	Grey	Grey	Aug 1955 to Sept 1955	G
Island Green	Green	Green	Aug 1955 to Dec 1958	T
	Black	Green		
Birch Grey	Grey	Grey	Sep 1955 to Aug 1956	B
	Maroon	Grey	Sep 1955 to Dec 1958	
Damask Red	Maroon	Red	Sep 1955 to Dec 1958	C
	Biscuit	Red		

Varitone Cars

Upper/Lower Colour	Seats and Trim	Carpet	Dates of Production	VIN Code
Birch Grey/ Twilight Grey	Maroon	Red	Oct 1956 to Dec 1958	BJ
	Grey	Grey		
	Biscuit	Red		
Ivory/Autumn Red	Biscuit	Red	Oct 1956 to Jan 1958	PC
	Maroon	Red		
Island Green/ Sage Green	Green	Green	Oct 1956 to Jan 1957	TE
	Black	Green		

Steel Blue/ Mineral Blue	Grey	Grey	Oct 1956 to Dec 1958	LD
	Black	Grey		
Ivory/Black	Maroon	Red	Oct 1956 to Dec 1958	PA
Birch Grey/Black	Grey	Grey	Oct 1956 to Dec 1958	BA
	Maroon	Red		
Island Green/ Black	Green	Green	Oct 1958 to Dec 1958	TA
Steel Blue/Black	Maroon	Grey	Nov 1956 to Dec 1958	LA
Island Green/ Reseda Green	Green	Green	Jan 1957 to Jan 1958	TE
	Black	Green		
Island Green/ Dark Green	Green	Green	Jan 1958 to Dec 1958	TU
	Biscuit	Green		
	Black	Green		
Kashmir Beige/ Wolseley Maroon	Maroon	Red	Feb 1958 to Dec 1958	FC
	Biscuit	Red		

The above colours were listed in sales literature. Records indicate a number of cars were produced in non-standard colours to special order.

Cars to Varitone specification (i.e. cars with the larger rear screen and full-length chrome trim) could be specially ordered in a single colour which could be any of those listed for the standard ZB or Varitone models. The VIN/chassis number assigned would have the same third and fourth letters: for example, the number for a Varitone-specification car finished all over in Island Green would begin KATT.

On early Varitones, wheels were painted to match the lower body colour. Later models had silver-painted wheels.

Bibliography

Allison, Mike, *The Magic of the Marque* (London: Dalton Watson, 1989).

Burgess, Peter, *How to Power Tune MGB four-cylinder Engines* (Veloce Publishing, 2013).

Clarke, R. M., *MG Cars 1955–1957* (Cobham: Brooklands Books).

Clausager, Anders Ditev, *MG Saloon Cars* (Bideford: Bay View Books, 1998).

Clausager, Anders Ditev, *Original MGA* (Bideford: Bay View Books, 1993).

Jacobs, Dick, *An MG Experience* (London: Transport Bookman Publications, 1976).

Lawson, John, *MG Y-type Saloons and Tourers* (Croydon: Motor Racing Publications, 1988).

McComb, F. Wilson, *MG* (London: Osprey Publishing, 1978).

Moylan, Brian, *Works Rally Mechanic* (Dorchester: Veloce Publishing, 1998).

Palmer, Gerald, *Auto-Architect* (East Horsley: Magna Press, 1998).

Shaw, Len, *Rallying in a Works MG* (East Horsley: Magna Press, 1997).

Smith, Philip H., *MG Series A and Magnette Tuning and Maintenance* (London: G. T. Foulis & Co., 1961).

Acknowledgements

The author and publisher would like to thank the following people/organisations for permission to use copyright material in this book. All references below are to photographs and other images:

Mike Allison: photographs from the Mike Allison collection of the Morris Cowley, Morris Sports Cowley, K3 Magnettes, Winners of 1933 Ards TT, MG 14/40 Salonette, MG Six saloon prototype exterior and interior and K1 Magnettes; The MG Car Club Archives: Cecil Kimber, the MG 14/40, 18/80, M-type Midget, WA saloon, MGF, Nancy Mitchell award presentation and ZB Magnette model; Vintage and Prestige Classic Cars Ltd: The MG 14/28 Super Sports Salonette (two pictures); Robin Lawton Vintage and Classic Cars: Riley 9 Monaco, Austin A90 Westminster exterior and engine, Magnette ZA with wire wheels; MG Car Club SVW Register: MG SA, VA and WA in line; MG Car Club Y-Register: Y-type production line; MG Car Club Magnette Register archives: Jan 1954 Magnette advert, *Air Trails Hobbies* July 1954 front cover, Oct 1956 Autosport Magnette advert, Manumatic transmission diagram, 1959 Magnette Mk III brochure, stock car racing pictures, Derrington advert, Lou Shorten and Lou & John Shorten, first Magnette Register meeting, Gordon Horner cartoon sketches; Celia Palmer: Gerald Palmer, Palmer's Model T Ford, Deroy sports car pictures, Riley Pathfinder, Palmer's Magnette sketch, Magnette press launch; Jowett Car Club Archive: Jowett Javelin prototype; Bianchi Anderloni Family Archives: Lancia Aprilia Aerlux (two pictures); and National Motor Museum, Beaulieu: Alfa Romeo 6C 2500, UFC 476 Magnette prototype, Gregor Grant's Magnette 1955 Monte Carlo Rally, Grant/Davis on 1956 Monte Carlo Rally, John Waller at Silverstone, 1955.

Every attempt has been made to seek permission for copyright material used in this book. However, if we have inadvertently used copyright material without permission/ acknowledgement we apologise and we will make the necessary correction at the first opportunity.

Many of the photographs in the book have been kindly provided by owners and enthusiasts. Sincere thanks are owed to Neil Cairns (Y-type saloon 438 LRM), Andrew de Bernes (V8 Magnette 406 ERG78), Andrew Brock (ZA Magnette 22 EMG), Alan Cleobury (Varitone TXF 336), Poul Dalkov (ZA Magnette A 487), Malcolm Eades (Darren

Brock's Mercedes-Magnette 225 FMK), David Halliday (ZB Magnettes GYE 450 and 594 AAF, Varitone YCO 260), Grant Howlett (ZA Magnette HGV 126), Colin Manley (MGA Twin-Cam), Warren Marsh (Gordon Horner cartoons), Peter Martin (Varitone 389 MMP), Kelly McClain (Lincoln-Zephyr), Noel Stokoe (Jowett Javelin FFR 900) and Dominic Taylor-Lane (ZB Magnette 94 LMH).

In addition, I would like to thank most sincerely the many people who have given freely of their time and expertise in helping me to write this book. In particular I should mention Mike Allison (vintage and Triple-M MGs), Giovanni Bianchi Anderloni (Carrozzeria Touring Superleggera), Alastair Clements (*Classic* and *Sports Car Magazine*), Val Foster (Wolseley 4/44), Peter Martin (historian, MGCC Magnette Register), Peter Neal (MG Car Club archives) and Celia Palmer (daughter of Gerald Palmer).

Finally, I thank my wife, Sarah Tenant-Flowers, not only for her patience as I have researched and written this book, but also for her fortitude over three decades, travelling many thousands of miles in the UK and across Europe in my 1956 ZA Magnette!